UNTAMED DEVOTIONS

STORIES OF A WILD GOD

Untamed Devotions

Stories of a Wild God

Shane Allen Burton

RADIANT HEART PRESS
MILWAUKEE, WISCONSIN

Published by
Radiant Heart Press
An imprint of HenschelHAUS Publishing, Inc.
www.henschelHAUSbooks.com

ISBN: 978159598-311-4
E-ISBN: 978159595-312-1
LCCN: 2014938351

Cover design by Lisa Marek of Fat Cat Art Studio , LLC

Printed in the United States of America.

I dedicate this book to my soul-mates.

My soul recognizes yours. I see you. You know me...my heart. This book really is for you. Because you've taught me that Love is not simply a choice one makes, but a deep feeling when one eternal soul recognizes itself in another. It is overwhelming, consuming, infinite, and completely, utterly, ridiculously wonderful. Thank you for teaching me to Love, and for Loving me in return. Thank you also for teaching me that Love comes from the Light, and a true Love relationship must exist as such.

For a book to be about Love and for one not to know the feeling would be a collection of empty words and platitudes. Thank you for awakening my soul to the glory of Love in all its splendor.

Thank you for teaching me about the heart of God.

Thank you as well for reminding me of God's Love in a time when I'd forgotten its Glory and Grace.

I also dedicate this book to my children: Patrick Riley, Tucker William, Darby Anne, and Zander Grey, whom I hope, above all else, know how very much I Love each of them. I am proud of you for who you are. And I send you the same invitation: take down your walls, remove your masks. You don't need to pretend to be anyone else than who you are.

You are amazing. Truly.
I Love you.

TABLE OF CONTENTS

ACKNOWLEDGMENTS

First of all, I have to recognize a few people who inspired this all to begin with: Russ and Kathy, Craig and Kari, Jed and Karin, Karen, Karla and Michelle. Without each of you asking, pushing, prodding, and challenging, this would never have happened.

Secondly, I need to acknowledge J.M. Dare, whose book I had the privilege of editing. For it was in editing her book, *36 Sense: Knowing You're Never Alone,* that I became encouraged to publish my own. J.M., you are a true friend in every sense of the word. Thank you for your story, trust, encouragement, and occasional smacks upside the head. I thank God for you.

Next, I want to thank Lisa Marek of Fat Cat Art Studio, LLC for her faithfulness, encouragement, accountability, and for being so ridiculously talented in translating my ramblings of what I hoped for in a cover design, into the work of art you hold in your hands, dear reader. Thank you, Lisa. You are an artist and a friend. I am grateful for the gift you are.

A special thanks as well to my sisters, Kammi and Denise. Thank you for cheering me on even though I probably didn't deserve it sometimes. You guys are the best! And to my dad, Royal: in so many ways, I am who I am because of you. You never let me settle, Dad. You pushed me to excellence. I thank you for that. I Love you.

I must also thank my band of brothers: Mike Graham: for pushing me, blessing me, and being Irish. Jack

Jorgensen: so many adventures, so little time to recount them all (road graders, OA, Philmont, Mountain T.O.P., Florida, etc.)! And Darwin Stahlback: friends since elementary school from burnt sienna corduroys and the stick game, to your wedding and working projects together as adults. Jeff Eberhard: for all things Prince-related, for your encouragement, our adventures, and for being the awesome Jeffie that you are. Without each of you, I would not be the man I am today. Thank you for being iron sharpeners.

I must also mention and thank Tree, Doug, and Amy, Kevin and Jodi., Joel and Nikki, Jerry Lee, Brittney and Corey, Carol, Beth, Kristin, Rachel and Tony, Lisa D., Al, Pat and Erika, John L., Cindy D., Sean and Janae, Eric M., Paul and Deb, Josh and Kara, Dave H., Jared R., Heather P., Jared P., Sue, Earl and Sue, Erik and Amy, Pam and Byron, Erin, Caitlyn, Caleb, Jim and Stacy, Andy and Michelle, Todd and Dee, Jolane, Dennis O., and so many others. I know I'm forgetting to mention some names. Just know I thank God for you!

And finally, to my publisher, Kira Henschel. Thank you for taking the musings of my heart and helping distribute them to a wider audience...for taking a dream and making it a reality. Thanks for helping to spread the Love!

PREFACE

All you need is Love.
-John Lennon

I did not set out to write a book. A long time ago, a group of friends asked me for some inspirational writings. I started writing and sending out several each week to an email distribution list. After a few weeks, I asked my friends what they thought. They liked what I was sending, but informed me they thought I was just going to find them each a book, not write my own.

And thus this work began.

I will tell you this: my theology—or beliefs about God—has become radically simplified over the years. Do I believe Jesus was who he said he was? In short, yes. But when he was asked to sum up everything, he broke it down into two very short sentences:

Love God.

Love people.

That's it.

And that, dear reader, is the core of my belief system: we ought to magnify and spread Love in this world. Love is the primary force in this Universe. It is written about, sung about, agonized over, and celebrated more than anything else in all of human history. It is the highest of human experiences.

For when we Love, we echo the heart of God.

I invite you into these pages to search for Love in your life. Some of these are personal stories of real experiences. Some are allegorical. In some, I bare my soul. And maybe, some words will lay yours bare as well.

Hear me clearly: I am a hypocrite. I do not claim to be perfect. I've sinned, and boldly so. The very things I know I should not do, I sometimes do. I resonate with all of the messed up people God chose to use: murderers, adulterers, tax collectors, prostitutes, and fishermen, for these are my people...my tribe.

I think if we people of faith more openly admitted our hypocrisy and our imperfections, more people would consider being people of faith.

Allow the walls to fall. Take off the masks. No more pretense. Just Love.

That's why I wrote this book: to encourage you along the way to Love and be Loved.

I'm foolish enough to believe if we all choose to Love one another, we will change the world. But it starts here. It starts now.

It starts with me.

It starts with you.

Shall we begin?

Woo Hoo!

Philippians 4:4

arc Huser was his name.

Whenever I think of Marc, tears immediately come unbidden to my eyes, a little smile turns up at the corner of my mouth. Marc's voice was high-pitched... almost a squeak. His eyes sparkled the joy that abided in his heart. Marc laughed a lot. Marc always had a smile and always had something cheerful to say. I'll never forget the first time I met him. There he was, smile on his face and a crop of red hair that had grown wild on top of that freckled face. Marc had the kind of smile that when you see it, you just can't help but to join in. Infectious doesn't begin to describe it. When you walked into a room and saw Marc Huser's smile, you caught an incurable case of smiling as well.

Marc had this idea that I drove through terrible rush-hour traffic every day I would see him. And so often, the first question he would ask me was: "How was Spaghetti Junction?" a notoriously dangerous area of traffic in the Minneapolis area, known for accidents and traffic jams. Often, I was rushing in, frustrated and impatient, and his question about Spaghetti Junction only reminded me of my short drive. Ah, but then I'd see Marc's smile and all thoughts of frustration would fade.

Whenever I would leave Marc, he would call out to me: "Shane?"

"Yeah, Marc."

"*Hasta la vista,*" {dramatic pause}"*baby!*"

For those of you who know me, the words "Woo hoo!" are of frequent usage in my vocabulary. What you don't know is the source. When I would be with Marc, he would often ask what we were going to do that day. And most of the time, he would respond with a "Woo hoo!"

"Shane, what are we going to do today?"

"Well, Marc, I think we're going to the park." I would answer.

"Woo hoo!" Marc would respond.

The next day he'd ask again, "Shane, what are we going to do today?"

"Well, Marc, we're going to eat oatmeal and watch T.V," I would answer.

Again, Marc would respond, "Woo hoo!"

A tear again forms in my eye as I think back upon my days with Marc. You see, Marc lived a life of celebration. Every day to Marc was a marvel. Marc reveled in each moment. He reveled in waking. He reveled in sleeping. He reveled in watching T.V. He reveled in eating oatmeal. He reveled in taking a bath. And Marc reveled in God.

Marc was a spiritual guide for me, now that I think of it. At the time, I wasn't all too sure about all of the God details in my life. I was pretty sure there was one. But I wasn't sure of too many details. Marc was sure. And Marc lived his life, his all-too-short life, constantly in God's presence, reveling.

What I haven't told you is that Marc had hydro-encephalitis and was developmentally disabled. His head was huge because of the fluid that would build up more and more each day, forcing his skull to enormous proportions, placing terrible pressure upon his brain. They tried to place a shunt and drain the fluid. But it would only temporarily solve the problem. Marc's head just kept on growing, the fluid building up, and his poor body wasting away, atrophy gnawing at his muscles.

I worked with Marc to try to help him have some dignity. I got him up in the morning, bathed him, dressed him, combed his hair, and then helped him eat breakfast, and get out the door to school. I could have done all of this in about half the time it took me. But I wanted Marc to be as independent as possible. I wanted him to be able to do as much as he could on his own.

And I also wanted to spend time with Marc, basking in the glow of his smile, reveling along with him to the joy of being in God's presence. I didn't know it at the time, but Marc stood on Holy Ground all day, every day. Even though he couldn't stand at all, there he stood reveling in the presence of Love...of God.

I always knew there was something different about Marc. His smile was a reflection of the true celebration taking place daily in his heart. A smile I would only know for a short time.

Marc did not live very long. He was seventeen years old when he died. And as I sit here with tears streaming down my face, I can clearly see the celebration that took place when Marc Huser walked for the first time in years down streets of gold. Marc would have leaped into the air, a smile lighting up his face. Marc looked and saw God coming toward him. And Marc would have run to meet him.

God asked, "So Marc, how was the traffic on the way here?"

"God, Spaghetti Junction was terrible!" says Marc.

"Marc, I'm so glad you're here." says God.

"Woo hoo!" responds Marc.

My dear friend, when is the last time you reveled in Love...in God? When's the last time you realized the marvel of this very moment in which you're living? When is the last time you realized that celebration Love that God has for you?

When's the last time you shouted out a "Woo hoo!" of your own?

Marc Huser is a witness to the celebration Love that God has for us. Marc is a witness to the life of reveling, the party-life that awaits us. Let go of all that is so grown-up within you that stops you from letting that "Woo hoo" rip. Go for it. Right now. Wherever you are. Let it out. You know it's there...bunched up inside you from disuse. Dust off your "Woo hoo!" Stand up; revel in God, and let your "Woo hoo!" rip.

I praise God today for the faith of a child, who taught me to have the faith of a child.

Hasta la vista, Marc! Until I see you again...*baby*!

AN EAGLE'S KNOWLEDGE

Isaiah 40:28-31

*D*aylight breaks upon the rim of your aerie. In the distance, you see mighty cumulonimbus clouds, signaling a coming storm. The day promises adventure. You stand in your nest, and stretch your mighty wings to their fullest, basking in the new rays of the dawn.

As the eagle, you are the proudest of creatures. Your eyes see things no other can. You discern subtleties, where others see only generalities. Your plumage is black, showing not only your beauty, but your dignity. You wear a breastplate and crown of purest white, declaring to all your power and royalty. And why not? Your aerie stands in the highest of trees, far above any other bird's nest or animal's den. Your keen gaze scans the horizon of the realm of your rule. At the most distant edge of your sight, you discern a small breeze forming in the leaves of a mighty oak.

It comes.

Letting go with a fierce cry, you launch yourself from the rim of your aerie, your mighty wings beating down the dead breezeless air below them. You begin your search for the legendary thermal, the very Breath of God. But you do not feel its awesome power yet. You continue to flap your mighty wings in defiance of this stillness. And then the first taste of the breeze wafts across your azure eyes. You close them for just a second, breathing in the exquisite taste of the wind. You open your eyes to see the storm rapidly approaching in the distance.

You fear your search for the Breath of God may be cut short today. But still onward you flap your wings. Far below, you sense the stillness of a forest that knows a storm approaches. Your other brothers and sisters have taken shelter. And yet, you fly on in your quest to discover the Breath of God. What drives you? What motivates you to continue in flight? What is so special about the Breath of God?

Again you close your eyes, remembering the day when you heard Grandfather Eagle tell you of the time when he was borne aloft by the Breath of God. He told you that day of his great fear, but also of the intense ecstasy of communing with God through his Sacramental Breath. You remember the joy of Grandfather Eagle as he told you that story. You remember the tear that streamed forth from his fierce, tender gaze as he looked upon you and said, "Young Eagle, someday you will search for the Breath of God just as I did. On that day, you will have to remember three things: You must stop the beating of your wings, you must stop looking with your eyes, and you must feel with your soul."

"But Grandfather," you protest, "surely I will plummet as a rock to the earth or crash into a cliff or tree?"

Grandfather Eagle smiles with wisdom and says, "But so it must be if you are to soar upon the Breath of God."

Your young brain did not comprehend it then, nor does it understand yet today. You continue to beat your wings against the ever increasing Wind. It is no longer a Breeze. It has graduated to Wind. Briefly, you begin to fear that this Wind is the Breath of God. But you find no ecstasy within it. You do not understand how the joy of

Grandfather Eagle could be found in striving against the gale-force of this Wind.

You are the bravest of eagles. You are the mightiest of raptors, and yet, even your wings begin to tire in these gusts. Questions assail you. As your wings beat down upon the Wind, Doubt beats at the edges of your prudence. Should I be doing this? Do I have the strength? What was I thinking? Why should I continue on? And the final cry of your soul rips through the howling of the Wind around you: "Where are you, God?"

The Wind has become too strong for even you. Your wings have become weak as an eaglet's. Tears of frustration and fear begin to burst forth from your once fierce gaze. The frenzy of the Wind denounces your last vestige of confidence and you begin to fear certain death. You start to believe that your once proud form will end up smashed upon the rocks below. And as you come to the point of futility, you hear the words of Grandfather Eagle come gently forth from the recesses or your memory: "Young Eagle, someday you will search for the Breath of God just as I did. On that day, you will have to remember three things: You must stop the beating of your wings, you must stop looking with your eyes, and you must feel with your soul."

"No!" You scream into the cold Wind. "I can't just let go, Grandfather. I can't. I can't just let go. I can't just give up. I have to find the Breath of God, as you did. I will do it by strength, Grandfather. I will find it." But even as you utter these words, you realize the foolishness of what you say. Sobs of frustration and despair wrack your body. Even at this moment of utter futility, and unbeknownst to you, your pride stands between you and the Breath of God.

But sometimes the Wind is stronger than our pride and blows past it.

You have become too weak to flap. With a sob of finality, your wings beat no more. This is it. Your form continues forward for a brief moment, high above the rocky terrain. But then you begin to fall. You pick up speed as your pitiful form hurtles towards the ground. At this moment, you are the complete opposite of what you were this morning as you stood with dignity upon the rim of your aerie.

As you fall, only one question passes through your consciousness, "Where are You, God?" Over and over, you hear yourself asking, "Where are You, God? Where are You, God? Where are You, God? Where are You, God..."

And then you feel it. A hint of a heat ruffles your feathers. "Where are You, God? Where are You, God? Where are You, God? Where are You, God..."

It was almost too brief to notice, but then you feel it again. And this time, you feel something stir deep within you. The heat does not touch simply your feathers, it tickles your soul. The ground is speeding to meet you and claim your death in its embrace. You have come to a point of knowing there is nothing left within you that can make the difference. But this hint of heat against the tips of your wings reminds you again of Grandfather Eagle's words. What was the first part again? Oh yeah, stop the beating of your wings. Well, you did that a while ago. That's why you're plummeting at this very moment.

But Grandfather's words continue to come unbidden, "Next, close your eyes." What else do you have to lose at this point? What will it hurt to surrender to the Wind? With abandon, you close your eyes, knowing this will mean certain death. You pitch recklessly into the howling of the Wind, abandoning yourself to it. "Feel with your soul, Young Eagle." What does this mean? Grandfather! What did you mea...

There it is again. The heat of something you've never felt before brushes past you. You stretch your wings to touch it and...

And as a Summer Breeze fills a sail to propel a boat forth into the Great Sea, so does the Wind, which has now become the Breath of God—the *Ruach Elohim*—envelop your wings. As suddenly as you fell, you now ascend into the Sky. A laugh breaks forth from within. Joy. Pure, unadulterated Joy breaks forth as the Dawn did this very morning. You soar up and up and still further upwards into the clouds. You are One with the Breath of God. You commune with him in his Sacramental Wind. You realize now, that the Torrential Wind, and the Breath of God are one in the same. The Wind fierce and mighty. The Breath strongly gentle. And at this moment, you realize the wisdom of Grandfather Eagle.

It was only when you were willing to abandon yourself into the Wind that you were able to discover the Breath of God. Only when you were able to lay aside pride and accept death that you were able to find yourself and life. The futility of your pride brings forth a wave of shame. Again you sob. But this time, you sob out of the Love you feel for God. You sob with shame for the many ways in which you thwarted God's Breath from bearing you further aloft than you ever could have attained on your own. And as you sob these tears of shame, you feel a wave of warmth surge over you as you are borne even higher, up, up through the clouds, to the place where the Son dawns across the horizon of the cloud landscape.

You have died to the Eagle you once were. Your hope is now in the God who bears you up upon his very Breath. The shame gives way again to Joy. And a new strength surges within you. As you soar here above everything you know, you realize the tremendous gift you have just received. You realize the Source of your strength. You realize the great Joy of God. You realize a new destiny.

And so finally you return to your aerie. It's height is not so high anymore. But no matter. As you stand upon its rim, still embracing your newfound Joy, a young eaglet flies over towards you and inquires as to where you've been.

You can't help but to laugh at the irony of this moment. You invite the young eaglet over. You tell him that you have just been borne upon the Breath of God.

He asks, "Where may I find this Breath, sir?"

"Well, my young friend, there are three things you need to know..."

HEY, GOD...IF YOU'RE GOING TO SPEW, SPEW INTO THIS!

Revelation 3:14-15

As a kid, I puked a lot. And it was such a casual thing for me. I'd be outside running and playing with my friends. "Hey guys, hold on a sec." {barf}
"Okay, that's much better."

And I'd continue playing as if nothing had happened. Or I'd be at a lake swimming with my family and I'd accidentally swallow some water and {barf} there I'd go again. Biting into a brownie was always interesting. To learn whether a brownie had nuts in it, all you had to do was watch me for a couple of seconds after I'd bitten into it. If I barfed, that meant there were nuts.

While traveling with my family to Vermont, we stopped at a late-night cafe for some supper. I ordered a grilled cheese sandwich. Did you know they use different kinds of cheese in different parts of the country? Well, apparently out east, they use Swiss cheese. One bite. That's all it took for me to have to make a run for the restroom. Of course, I didn't do any resting in there.

Another time, my cousin Jon was over to our house for dinner and my mom, in her infinite wisdom, decided to try a new vegetable on us. She was always trying to find vegetables that I would eat. Brussels sprouts were not one of them. This was the first time, though, that I had participated in the sport of synchronized projectile vomiting. Because as both my cousin and I took one bite of one Brussels sprout, our gag reflexes immediately gave indication to my parents that Brussels sprouts would not soon become a regular part of our diets.

Often, my parents would have some friends over to play cards or games. They would sit around all night, talking, laughing, playing their games, and drinking gallons upon gallons of Coca-Cola. A favorite past time of any child is to stealthily approach their parents' glasses and, while they're not looking, guzzle as much as possible, replacing said glass before anyone is the wiser. My sister and I were very good at this. We even learned to be able to hide the noisy chug and gasp sounds most children make when engaging in these covert ops. The carbonation in Coke is too strong for most kids. Not us. We were good. We had engaged in strict training to condition our throats to be able to handle the extreme acidity and carbonation present in ice-cold Coca-Cola.

After everyone would leave, my sister and I would often go around drinking the remainder of each person's glass. We weren't aware of backwash or germs yet. Nor did we really care. Mom and dad didn't let us drink Coke. So we would get our hands on the stuff any way we could. Usually, by this time in the evening, all of the Coke was pretty watered down from all of the ice that had been added. Perfect for guzzling. There were some nights when we probably each scored a couple of liters a piece. {Sigh} Those were the days.

I will never forget one time, however, when my parents went to bed without cleaning up after their little soiree. I woke up at my usual time, 6:00am. I went out to the dining room and lo and behold, to my wondering eyes did appear were 6 half-empty cans of Coke and 2 empty cans of beer. With an excited grin, I was lively and quick, and I began guzzling, but soon knew I'd be sick. For the half-empty cans were warm to the touch, and I threw up often, and I threw up much.

The pop was lukewarm and it was nasty. It made me spew.

And that's exactly what God says he'll do if we live lukewarm lives. Lukewarm is mediocre. It's beige. It's safe. It's neither hard nor soft, fire or ice, infrared or ultraviolet.

God, of course, would prefer to see lives that are on fire! These are people that are bold bearers of Love in a hurting world. These are people that come with food in one hand and grace in the other. These are people who take Love with them wherever they go. These are people who consider everywhere they go to be a mission trip. When they go to the store, it's a mission trip. When they go to work, it's a mission trip. When they volunteer in their child's class in school, it's a mission trip. Everywhere these people go, they see opportunities to share Love with the least, the last and the lost.

These are the kinds of lives God Loves to see. But he says here that he'd prefer people to be ice-cold, rather than lukewarm. How can that be? That doesn't seem to make sense. Or does it?

Ice-cold lives are the ones that have lost their fire entirely. They're dead...lifeless. But what business is God in? God is in the Life Insurance business, providing resurrection to those who are dead! Hello! God would prefer an ice-cold life, because God is in the business of fire-breathing and life-bringing. God promises the gift of Love, and whenever Love shows up, bring your marshmallows, 'cause there's going to be a fire!

But the lukewarm lives are those who remember what it's like to be on fire, and yet they're either too afraid or too comfortable to do so. They're afraid because if they're on fire, then things are going to burn out of control. And lives that are lukewarm have serious control issues. And control issues always come out of a sense of fear.

Or else they're too comfortable, and in which case, they've grown complacent. Comfort always breeds complacency. And complacency breeds apathy. Pretty soon, you have a life that vaguely remembers its glory-days of being on fire, but has no will to put any energy into being that kind of a life again, and so at best, they will occasionally try something new, thinking that will echo the glory of the good ol' days. The new thing will actually fool them into thinking they are a life on fire and they will strut around, mimicking passion.

Mimicked passion is primordial luke-warmness. {Barf}

So, how's your life? Have you taken your temperature lately? When you taste of your life, is it hot? Is it cold? Or is it lukewarm? Hot would be great. It means that your life is taking the Commission given to us to Love one another seriously.

If your life is cold, it means that you're ripe for revival. All it takes is for you to decide that today is the day. Today is the day when you are going to "get busy living," as Red said in The Shawshank Redemption.

And if you're lukewarm...ouch.

God says, however, that there is still hope for a lukewarm life. That hope is born from Loving. If a lukewarm life begins to Love with abandon, that is a life that will soon burn again.

It will be hard...probably much harder than the revival an ice-cold life will experience. But it will be worth it. It will mean trading in comfort for dis-comfort. It will mean trading in security for risk. It will mean trading in our threadbare rags and fool's gold, for the finery and wealth that can only come from Love. It means trading in our snake-oil programs for Life-bringing faith.

Are you ready? Are you ready for this kind of a life? Are you ready to let go of comfort so you can be uncomfortable? Oh, I sure hope so, my friend. You won't regret it. The best rides in life are never free and they're never comfortable. There's always a cost. And they're always hot!

By the way, my stomach doesn't plague me nearly as much as it used to. I guess I've learned more about what affects me adversely and how to avoid such things.

Let us, however, not avoid Love, so that Love will not avoid us.

NEW HOPE RISING

2 Corinthians 4:16-18

*M*y uncle was a bowler. I'm talkin' like Fred Flintstone here. He had his own bowling ball, bowling ball bag, and even his own bowling shoes. He would not be caught dead in those ugly red and green bowling shoes. No, he wore nice bowling shoes with comfortable soles and arch support.

While my uncle was a bowler, I was a budding scientist. In science, you test hypotheses. At the age of five, I was watching an episode of Mr. Roger's Neighborhood—in which they took a bowling ball and cut it in half with a band saw. They showed us that the center of a bowling ball was filled with cork.

In an episode of the cartoon, Tennessee Tuxedo (the smart-sounding penguin who was actually stupid with the dumb-sounding walrus sidekick named Chumley, who was actually smart) they escaped, yet again, from the zoo to go and see Mr. Whoopee. Mr. Whoopee had all of the answers to all of the questions. And he also had a magic chalkboard that would bring images to life.

Whenever Tennessee and Chumley went to see Mr. Whoopee, they would come prepared with a question and Mr. Whoopee would go and retrieve his chalkboard from his closet and begin to sketch their answer. Mr. Whoopee had a closet crammed full, like the Tupperware cupboard in my kitchen. Every time our heroes came with a question, Mr. Whoopee's closet would empty out its contents onto the seemingly unsuspecting Mr. Whoopee.

In one episode, Tennessee and Chumley needed to know about directions. And so Mr. Whoopee explained to them the intricacies of North, South, East, and West and then told them about compasses. He told them they could make a homemade compass out of a cork and a needle.

If you take the needle, and drop it on the floor, it will make it magnetic. Then you poke the needle through the cork and float the cork in a small cup of water. Cool, huh? I've tried it. It works. It's not the snappiest compass in the world, but if you're patient, you'll find North.

So, in my budding scientific brain, a hypothesis was forming: cork floats, bowling balls have cork centers, soooo...bowling balls will float!

The only way to discover if your hypothesis is fact or fiction is to test it. So we did. I found my lab assistants, my three- and four-year-old cousins, and we hijacked my uncle's bowling ball. My cousins lived on a small, sloping hill that had a pond at the bottom of it. And it wasn't the kind of a pond that had a nice sloping shoreline. This pond dropped straight down almost ten feet (as I remember it...it was probably like three feet...but hey, I was five...seemed more like an ocean to me).

Are you getting the picture of what came next? The bowling ball was pretty heavy for us little squirts. But you know, with the help of the hill and a little Newtonian force known as gravity, the ball was propelled easily into the murky waters of our oversized Petri dish. Thooooommp! The water hardly even splashed; so perfectly spherical was the glossy surface of the subject of our experiment. It was glorious. We danced around like natives after a kill. We reveled in the glory of the moment!

And then we realized something. The ball was not coming back up.

Words cannot fully express the feeling in that moment. Terror hints at it. We didn't really have a grasp on profanity yet. However, we did not really know such words and so we uttered a simple, but effective, "Oops."

In that moment, my cousins looked at me as if I were a dead man. They knew the wrath of their father was going to descend. And they knew that it would not be upon them. They would let me suffer the consequences on my own. After all, it was my hypothesis, right? I tried to convince them that we were all a part of a team...a glorious team...that was working toward the betterment of humanity. They didn't buy it. They simply pointed their fingers at me as if to say, "He did it." And fifteen minutes later, when we still did not see the bowling ball rising to the surface, that's exactly what they did when my aunt and mother came walking down the hill to see what we were up to.

"He did it!" they announced.

{Sigh} Such greatness of thought is always under appreciated.

My cousins had already given up on my hypothesis. And I'll admit, my hope was rapidly fading. But deep in my gut, I knew that if cork floated in small amounts, that it would certainly float in larger amounts and that while pigs may never fly, bowling balls indeed would float. Seemingly, everything was falling apart. The best-laid plans...well, you know...the looks on our mothers' faces said it all. We were dead. They were going to end our lives.

But there was more here than meets the eye. Because deep within the murky depths of the pond, something was occurring. The principle of buoyancy was being applied.

And the downward motion of the bowling ball had finally been reversed.

Slowly—oh so slowly—the bowling ball was rising to the surface of the pond! And as we were turning to go and receive our beatings, a small flicker of movement caught my eye. It could've been a frog or a small fish that was the source of the movement. But my heart said differently. My hope was renewed. A burst of energy surged within my body. My scientific hypothesis was about to be proven correct! Ha ha ha! A maniacal laugh spewed forth from my lips. And all gathered there upon that grassy hillside turned to see that which I was seeing.

The bowling ball was slowly rising to the surface! A cheer broke forth! My cousins were even a little excited. But secretly, I'm sure they were bummed that I was going to get out of this beating.

It took a week or so, but the bowling ball made it to the surface and was retrieved by the neighbors on the other side of the pond and then returned to my uncle. He received the bowling ball with great relief.

I was about to abandon hope. I was about to give up on that which I knew in my heart to be true. Everything on the outside of that situation said that things were falling apart. But on the inside of the pond, where I could not see, a new hope was rising.

We are all called to a personal mission or purpose in life. Mine is to build up leaders...to encourage people...to inspire...to train, equip, and raise up others to do the same. What's your mission on this planet? What is your purpose?

Maybe you need to start there? What excites you? What makes you angry? What moves you to tears? These questions may help you uncover your mission.

And once you know what it is, then you need to know there will be times when you will be discouraged in your progress. There have been so many times when I've felt things falling apart around me. I've looked around to find myself alone. I've looked at budgets and found them lacking. I've looked in the eyes of a person who is so burned out in life and has lost their sense of purpose that for personal health, they've needed to leave the mission for a while.

In these moments, I've almost abandoned hope. There have been times when giving up seemed to me a viable option. Everything on the outside seemed to be falling apart. In those moments, I was not trusting in what God was doing on the inside where I could not see.

I wasn't trusting that cork floated, and so would the bowling ball of my purpose.

Have you ever felt this way? Have you ever cried out to the Universe asking, "What's the point? Look, it's not going to float! Why are you having me wait around here for this mission if we both know it's going to sink? Hello? God? Are you there?"

I'm quite certain in these moments that God is smiling that I-told-you-so kind of a smile. And with said smile utters two words to us: "Trust me."

Notice that he did not say, "Trust you." He said, "Trust me."

And there's the crux of this whole matter. When we trust in ourselves, we will come up wanting. We will turn away from the pond of life, thinking that our personal purposes to which we've been called have sunk and become wrecks upon the bottom of life's pond to be explored eons hence by archaeologists who will shake their heads and say, "Tsk, tsk. It's too bad."

When we trust in God, we will wait at the water's edge with joyous expectancy, knowing that Love is at work all around us and is making New Life in and through our purpose on the inside, where we cannot see.

When the prodigal bowling ball surfaced and was returned to us, a celebration ensued! We whooped and yee-hawed. We had a celebration that greatly overshadowed the gloom of those moments when we thought all hope was lost. The hard times of the sunken bowling ball were small potatoes compared to the lavish celebration that was prepared for us when the bowling ball rose to the surface.

At this moment, you may be standing at the water's edge with joyous expectancy, knowing that God's working wonders on the inside. Or you may be about to turn away, abandoning hope.

My friend, hang on. Don't go. Wait.

Listen to the two words that God is speaking to you at this very moment: "Trust me. I'm doing things on the inside that you can't even begin to imagine. But they are wondrous and will bring great joy. Your purpose may not be rising as fast as you'd like it to be rising. But it's rising as fast as I'd like it to be rising. So don't turn around. Don't go. Don't give up. You know I've called you to this...so why would I let it fail? Do not let yourself be deceived by human standards of success. Your trust in my Love is all the success you'll ever need. Trust me."

Now, if you're living for a purpose to which you've not been called, the bowling ball may never resurface.

Deal with it and move on.

Look for Love at work around you. Listen to your heart when it begins to quicken with excitement. When you find your purpose, you will know. And when you know, you will also discover times when your purpose will be so challenging you will be tempted to give up. But don't turn away. It's coming. Don't give up hope. Your mission is rising—maybe not as quickly as you'd like—but it is.

We had another hypothesis: Bowling balls float, so wouldn't bowling shoes float as well?

Bowling shoes do not float. Trust me.

THE DESERT OF MY SOUL

Psalm 63: 1-2

I was born in the desert. Wherever I looked, it was arid and dusty. Moisture was precious and more of a dream than anything I regularly experienced. Life to me was a series of dunes, waves of sand, constantly shifting and re-shaping themselves with the gentle forces of wind, time, and tectonic movement.

I knew the sun. I knew wind. I knew endless days of trudging through a bleak oblivion. I knew pain. I knew the irritation of grains of sand, seeping into the crevices of my body and my soul. My eyes would sting and tear up with the grit of my existence.

However, in the midst of this desert, there was the occasional oasis. Oasis: a lush refuge in the midst of a wasteland. Along the way, I would occasionally encounter these. Rare would be an understatement as to the frequency of their occurrence. When I would happen upon them, I would race toward them, parched from thirst, my lips—my soul—cracked and bleeding from going so long without the blessing of moisture.

Upon entering the oasis, I would scramble to the water, look into it's mirrored surface, and then tentatively—for I was afraid the miracle would be a mirage—reach my hands out to disturb the glassy surface, feeling the water's cool caress on my parched skin. And after feeling the water's touch, I would cup my hands and I would scoop up some of the precious substance, bring it to my mouth, suck it in, and then just hold it there for a moment...eyes closed, head tilted back in the exaltation of the moment. That first swallow would wrack my body with tear-less sobs, for I was so dehydrated that tears were an impossibility. Relief...from the sun. Relief from the heat. Relief from the arid existence in which I wandered.

After drinking as much as I could, I would dive in, head first and I would flail about as a child, reveling in the great joy and beauty of the moment. Green leaves, lush grass, and delicious fruit would abound in these oases. And while I stayed, the rich environment would bless me tremendously.

Sometimes, I would venture forth, thinking I'd had my fill...believing I could once again manage the wasteland of desert that had become so familiar to me. For life couldn't truly be so lush, could it? Life shouldn't be so green and lush and vibrant, should it?

The desert had become my reality...my normality.

As in a dry and weary wasteland, I thirsted for something greatly. I would go from oasis to oasis with long stretches of desert wasteland in between. I knew that life was not supposed to be a blessing, but rather was to contain only occasional moments of blessing.

Sometimes I chose to leave the oases, believing in my own strength...believing in my own power. But all too soon, I would find myself stumbling about blindly with my eyes glued shut from tears, salt, and the grit of the desert, my lips cracked and bleeding, my skin burned raw and red from the sun and wind, hoping to happen upon another moment of miracle, yet all too often finding only the mirage.

Other times, I would stay too long in the oasis and use up its bounty until all that existed were a few dried up leaves and some cracked bits of mud...bitter reminders of what was.

And yet other times, fellow wayfarers would coax me out from my refuge, promising rivers, oceans, and rainforests. Some of these wayfarers, I believe, knew of what they spoke. They had been there. They had seen such things. They knew, from experience, that such Places existed. They spoke only the Truth...the vibrant, living, lush Truth.

Others, however, pointed the way to false images of water, idols of greener places. These wayfarers were bitter people who had been fooled by others. They were out to get me as they had been gotten themselves. They would fool me as they too had been fooled. They lured me forth with empty hopes and false promises. They spoke only the Lie...the listless, dead, arid Lie.

One day, in the midst of my wanderings, I realized I had been greatly deceived. And in that realization came hopelessness, depression, and apathy. I fell upon my knees, my insides clenching and churning. As spasms of despair began to shake my soul, I curled up within myself, locking away my heart, denying my need for water...my need for the Truth. I convinced myself that the Lie was Truth...sand was water...water, sand.

In a frenzy, I flew madly through the dunes, up one ridge, to its crest, believing the Lie to be Truth. For as far as I could see, the dunes stretched to the horizon. Nothing else existed. The Lie was Truth. I gave up. There was nothing to eat. There was nothing to drink. There was nowhere to go. There was no one to whom to turn. For even when I turned to those I knew, I didn't know the difference between Lie and Truth. Their words were gibberish to me.

I don't really know when it happened. All I know is that at one point, I heard a Voice telling me to go away. I needed to go away. I began to wander the desert again. But this time, I didn't even hope for an oasis. Instead, I simply abandoned myself to a direction and began to walk. It didn't matter to me which way I walked, for all ways led only to an endless expanse of wasteland...a wasteland that had become my home. But in that walking came a silence, and in that silence came a peace...and in that peace, the Voice spoke to me again.

"If you knew the generosity of Love and who I am, you would be asking me for a drink, and I would give you fresh Living Water."

I answered the Voice: "No. There is no such thing. There is sand. There is mirage. There is the Lie that is my truth. Living Water is an image on some madman's painting. It isn't Truth."

That night, I curled up in a ball, and cried myself to sleep. A single tear streaked down my dust-caked face...a river in the midst of that wasteland. It wasn't possible, but the remnant of that tear was still there in the morning. I felt the tickle of the single droplet, there on my cheek. I pondered at what the tickle was. And then I remembered my grief from the night before. I slowly brought one finger to my cheek and touched the droplet, then brought it to the tip of my swollen tongue. And something flickered in me in that moment.

Hope.

I remembered the sound of the Voice and remembered that it was a Voice to which I was not unfamiliar. It was a Voice, in fact, that I knew well, but somewhere along the way, had become garbled to me. For two more days, I wandered, listening for another Word from the Voice. And when I had almost given in to the Lie again, the Voice spoke to me and said simply, "Go."

And so I did. I went. I simply began to walk in one direction. I had something that I hadn't had in a long time. Hope. I remembered the tales of those wayfarers whose hearts seemed wholesome. I remembered how they spoke of rivers and oceans and rainforests. I remembered the Voice that promised me fountains of Living Water springing up within me...that I would never again be thirsty.

One day, I stumbled upon the edge of the desert. I tripped over it and fell face first into a vast expanse of moist, lush, green forest...dripping with drops from the latest downpour. Had I not stumbled, I think I would have turned away, believing it to be a mirage. Instead, I fell face-first into the Miracle.

Somewhere along the way, I had become convinced that life was supposed to be a desert with occasional oasis moments. I had become convinced that this Love-less land was my normality.

And then I fell face-first into a Love-rich land and realized the Lie I had come to believe as Truth. Truly, it was just like stepping from Dorothy's black and white house into the Technicolor Land of Oz.

It's an amazing thing to come to the edge of your desert and realize the rainforest promise of Love. Sometimes I can't believe how stupid I was to believe the Lie...to be convinced that the Truth was silly.

I believed that life was to be virtually void of feeling, with only occasional moments of joy...of Love. I needed to come to a place outside myself...outside my parameters...my controls...my knowledge...my experience. I needed to be stripped of everything to be given the one thing I needed most: Love...Living Water.

The wilderness times of life...those times in the desert are times when Love seems completely absent, but in reality, it's just out of our line of vision. It's there. But these are times of refining and growth. They're times when Love chooses to remain silent to grow your sense of hope through perseverance. It's easy to hope during the good times...when Love is obvious. But in the times when Love is quiet, how is your Hope?

If you're reading this and you know the desert of despair, all I can tell you is this: despair is not the Truth. There is a rainforest promise that awaits you. Your journey will be hard. It will be lonely at times if you choose to believe in the seemingly insane Promises of Love. But it's even lonelier when you don't.

Believe me. I've been there...

And now I'm back.

OBVIOUS QUESTIONS, OBVIOUS ANSWERS

John 21:15-20

My son comes up to me. It's 6:17 a.m. Me? I'm in my PJs, crazed hair, bleary eyes, desperately seeking coffee, thoughts sluggish. It is in this severely deprived state that my young son accosts me.

"Dad, can I have some chocolate?" he asks hopefully.

I start to answer "Sure, whatever."

But then the reality of what he has asked settles into my sub-cortex and I become aware of the circumstances that I will face if I allow the chocolate (certain death by clubbing at the hands of his mother). And so I say something brilliant like: "No...wait. No chocolate."

I have caught him just in time. But he is persistent. And he has the advantage. He is alert. I am not.

"Dad, how about some cookies?" He asks the question nonchalantly, making it sound as if he's asking for a bowl of fruit or a plate of okra. The inflection in his voice is misleading. The cookies almost sound nutritious to me in my haze of slumber.

Again, I falter for an answer, and just in time, I realize the question and the appropriate answer and simply murmur "No."

Ah, but the child is both persistent and patient. He waits for me to settle into a chair. He waits for my brain to begin to nod off once again into sleepy-land. If I were truly aware of my environment, I would notice the sunlight glinting off the drop of spittle hanging from the little fiend's fangs. He is crouched, waiting to pounce upon his poor, unsuspecting father with another precarious question, which, if answered incorrectly, will land his father in deep doo-doo with mommy.

Hold...hold...his muscles are taut with the energy of the pounce. He is ready. I am not.

"Dad, could I please have some chocolate milk?"

Now, any alert parent knows the obvious answer to this question. "No, of course you may not have chocolate milk...for breakfast!" It's a no-brainer. A duhhhh!

But I was not ready for the attack. I was caught unaware. I heard the polite "please" that the nice boy said, and I heard the word "milk." Somehow, my brain missed the "chocolate" part of the request. "Sure, whatever." I responded somewhat incoherently. My son, very excitedly, said, "Thanks, dad!" And he rushed off to pour his cereal...with chocolate milk.

After a while, I stumbled into the kitchen to make my morning cup o' Joe. I gathered my mug, the coffee and a pot-full of water and began. Within just a couple of minutes, a freshly brewed pot of extra-strength mud awaited my consumption. Light would not penetrate the depths of this coffee. I poured a cup, and began to sip on my morning brew.

As the fragrant java began to course through my consciousness, the haze began to recede and I turned to see my child—my darling sweet monster...er ahhh...child, look at me with eyes that said, "You said I could do this. And I'm tellin' mom." Sugarcoated loops of fruit, bathing in a bowl of chocolate milk. I would be a dead man, as soon as Mommy learned of this lapse of parental judgment.

Obvious questions with obvious answers.

The same was true with Jesus and Simon Peter in the little exchange we have in the last chapter from the story of Jesus' life as told by his youngest disciple, John. Jesus asks Peter obvious questions. "Peter, do you Love me?"

You can see the puzzled look on Peter's face as he wonders why Jesus is asking such an obvious question. The look says, "Okay, what's the catch? You know I Love you, Jesus." After waiting just a second to see if he can see what Jesus is up to, Peter answers, "Duh. You know I Love you, Jesus. Why are you asking such a silly question?"

So Jesus, being his ever-playful self, gives a rather cryptic answer. He says with a glint in his eye, "Feed my lambs." Can you see the way the corner of Jesus' mouth is upturned, a little grin forming there as he waits for Peter to get it?

But Peter ain't the sharpest tool in the shed. He leans forward just a bit, squinting through confused eyes at Jesus, thinking to himself, "Lambs? I didn't even know you had sheep." You can just about hear the crickets chirping in the background as Peter sits there confusedly looking at his grinning friend.

But Jesus is persistent. And he asks the question again rather nonchalantly, examining the fingernails of his left hand. "Peter, do you Love me?"

"Really!?" Peter almost shouts in frustration to the obvious enjoyment of Jesus. Peter sits there, wondering what's going on. Why is Jesus acting so weird? Why is he asking such stupid questions? And as Peter sits there wondering, his ire rises within him and he answers, rather frustrated, "Hello! Jesus, you, of all people, know that *I Love you.* Why do you ask?"

Jesus just grins openly this time. And he sits back on his haunches, enjoying the confusion on his friend's face. He waits before he answers with his enigmatic response, "Peter, shepherd my sheep."

And Peter sits there, still wondering about this illusive flock of sheep that he didn't know Jesus possessed. Peter actually begins to retrace their footsteps to try and figure out where this flock of sheep resides. Was it back in Galilee? What about over in Nazareth where Jesus was from? No matter how much brain he puts into it, he still can't figure out what Jesus is up to. He knows it should be obvious, at least it seems that way by the manner in which Jesus is both asking and answering. Peter is getting impatient and frustrated.

Ah, but Jesus is both patient and persistent. And he asks a third time, "Peter, do you Love me?"

"Arghh!" Peter lets out with a cry of pent-up frustration. "Jesus, after all we've been through...after all the places we've been, the demons we've kicked out, the sick we've healed, the imprisoned we've set free...after all this, you have to ask if I Love you? You know I Love you. Why do you have to ask me three times?"

This time, Jesus smiles a rueful smile as he waits for the words Peter has uttered to sink in. A moment spanning eons passes by. You can see the realization slowly creep down Peter's face. Tears well up in his eyes as he realizes that Jesus has asked three times if Peter Loves him.

Jesus gave Peter the chance to retract each of his three denials by proclaiming his Love for Jesus. There is an oft misunderstood and under-fathomed word for this.

Grace.

Obvious questions, with obvious answers to reveal what Jesus would like for his sheep to be so very obvious:

Grace. It is what Easter is all about. It is at the core of Jesus' message of Love. Grace: unwarranted and unmerited Love. Extravagant in nature. Wild. Untamed. Unrestrained. The passionate *eros* Love of Jesus for his rather dim-witted sheep.

And out of Grace, comes our charge: "Feed and shepherd my sheep. Take care of them. Love them, as I have Loved you. This Grace I extend to you, share with my sheep, Peter." And then Jesus grinned, you just know it. And he opened his arms for a hug. Peter sees the scars, a tear begins to form from sorrow and shame, but then he sees the grin, and the tear turns to joy as he embraces him in a Peter-sized bear hug.

The questions for you today are obvious, aren't they? Friend, do you know Love? And if you do, are you feeding any sheep?

My prayer for you is that your answers are equally obvious.

THE LOVE OF HIS HEART

Song of Songs 2:11-17

Some friends of mine decided to get married. They figured their enamor for one another was reason enough to get hitched. They selected this passage from the Song of Songs that talks about Love and passion as their wedding text. At this point, they had much to learn about each other, about Love, about marriage, and about God.

Besides the fact that they're dear friends, what makes their wedding so very memorable to me is not so much the wedding itself. Rather, it's the rehearsal dinner. Or should I say, the aftereffects of the rehearsal dinner.

Once the groom arrived at the rehearsal, (an hour late, for he had to finish his round of golf...you see what I mean about having much to learn?) we got started and things began to go much more smoothly. Fun was had by all as we practiced the steps they would take down the aisle. And as two people in Love should do, they looked deeply into one another's eyes and practiced the vows they would say the next day in that same spot, with a whole lot more fanfare and pomp.

As I tell every couple I'm going to marry, "Look, as long as you both show up tomorrow, and I show up, we can always grab a couple of witnesses off the street and still have a wedding. Everything beyond that which goes smoothly is gravy. If the cummerbunds all match, if the dresses all fit, if all who are supposed to show up actually show up—that's all gravy...a bonus. What will live long after tomorrow is not the wedding, but the marriage."

In literary terms, what we're talking about here is called foreshadowing.

It was the chicken. For the rehearsal dinner, we had these very yummy baked chicken breasts. We were in a dimly lit room, candles glowing, champagne flowing and as I cut into my chicken breast, I thought I noticed a slight shade of pink, indicating to my father-who-is-a-butcher-trained eyes the chicken was not fully cooked. And if you know anything about uncooked chicken, you know better than to eat it.

I convinced myself that such a fine restaurant would make sure the chicken was fully cooked. In fact, not only did I eat one under-cooked chicken breast...I went for two.

And it was around two in the morning that I realized the error of my ways as I made my way rapidly through the dark to the bathroom to purge myself of the poisonous food I had ingested. In fact, I kept on purging until around nine. It was an early afternoon wedding as I recall. I was beginning to question my ability to perform my friend's wedding. By ten, I was able to hold down a can of Coke. A quick burst of caffeine and sugar energy, giving me the illusion of strength. I gently gulped down a couple of more cans and voila. I deemed myself ready to perform the ceremony.

The wedding went off without a hitch. The groom was on time. I'm certain he'd have been offed by some member of the bride's family, if not the bride herself had he been late. I made it through. I was only woozy a couple of times, but a deep breath or two and I was fine.

Their marriage started off in the middle of a spiritual winter. It was faced with challenges. In fact, the wedding itself almost didn't happen because of a late groom and a very ill pastor. The winter that faced their marriage was bitter and foxes were hungry and roaming, ready to pounce.

Some say the *Song of Songs* is about God's example of how a Love relationship ought to be: passionate, caring for one another, and filled with Love. I think that's probably true.

Others say it's about God's relationship with us. Does it weird you out to think that God wants to have a passionate relationship with us? It kind of did me at first. Until I started to grow deeper in my relationship with God, I had only the *agape* Love understanding of God. Agape Love is that sterile "I Love you in God's way" (air quotes) kind of Love we used to joke about as kids. It's an altruistic Love that serves the other, not the self. Agape Love is only a subtle shade of God's Love.

The *Song of Songs* speaks in the terms of *eros* Love. It is the Love of passion. And I believe that God is passionately in Love with us. Read the passage from the Song of Songs again, but this time, hear God saying the words of The Man to you and respond back to God with the words of The Woman as your prayer.

God: "Look around you! Winter is over; the winter rains are over, gone! The dark times of waiting and wondering are past. Spring flowers are in blossom all over. The whole world's a choir—and singing! Spring warblers are filling the forest with sweet arpeggios. Lilacs are exuberantly purple and perfumed, and cherry trees fragrant with blossoms. Oh, get up, dear friend, my fair and beautiful Lover—come to me! Come, my shy and modest dove—leave your seclusion, come out in the open.

Let me see your face, let me hear your voice. For your voice is soothing and your face is ravishing. I want to hear from you. I want to hear your voice. I want to hear about your day. I want to know your fears and calm them. I want to hear your hurts and soothe them. I want to see your dreams and help you to realize them. I want to dance through life with you, every day a celebration. Won't you talk with me? Won't you share your heart with me...give it to me?"

You: "Then you must protect me from the foxes, foxes on the prowl, foxes who would like nothing better than to get into our flowering garden. You are mine, and I am yours. Nightly you stroll in our garden, delighting in the flowers until dawn breathes its light and night slips away. Turn to me, dear Lover. Come like a gazelle. Leap like a wild stag on delectable mountains! I would gladly give you my heart, but I am afraid of the foxes who prowl, waiting to pounce upon me when I am vulnerable."

God: "I understand your fear, dear one. Yes, the foxes are out there and they are always ready to pounce. But as long as you walk in our garden with me, their attacks will be nothing in the face of my Love for you. Evil is always waiting, watching for any sign of weakness and will continue to prowl in the bushes, trying to distract you from me."

You: "I will try. I will try to surrender my fear to you, dear one. I will try to trust in you only as we walk together in the garden. And I will try as well to talk more with you."

God: "That is good to hear."

You: "I have a question for you, friend."

God: "Yes, my dear one."

You: "Why is the winter so long? Why do you allow the foxes to prowl?"

God: "That's two questions. But I will answer them because I Love that we are talking. Why is the winter long? It teaches you to trust me. It teaches you that our Love for each other must be strong enough to carry us through the winter times of life. It teaches you that our Love cannot simply delight in *good feelings*.

"Your Love for me must go deeper than that. To be faithful when times are tough is true faithfulness. To be faithful when we delight in one another isn't that difficult is it? And why do I allow the foxes to prowl? Because I know our Love is stronger and because I allow you to choose. It's quite a powerful gift, isn't it, the gift of choice? But without it, your Love for me wouldn't be Love, would it? I must allow you to choose the path of the Fox, or the path that I have prepared for us to walk on together."

You: "You must trust me an awful lot."

God: "It is because of my passionate Love for you, dear one."

You: "I Love you."

God: "I Love you, too."

SPIRITUAL REDHEADS

John 8:7
Ephesians 3:5

Only three percent of the world's population has red hair. Did you know that? I look like a leprechaun. I've been told it a thousand times. There's pretty much no escaping my DNA. I'm short. I'm stocky. I'm a redhead. Hey, I'm Irish.

When this Irishman was but a wee lad, we moved to a new neighborhood. I believe I was four years old when we moved. It was just before kindergarten started, so I turned five that summer. While I was playing one day, I met one of the kids in the neighborhood. His name was John Held. We hit it off famously and soon became good friends.

I knew that John had other friends. But I never played with them. Not because I didn't want to, but because they told me I was different. John and I became better friends. We played often. We ran through the neighborhood, pretending to be Batman and Robin. We invented machines that would create delicious concoctions and also fly us to Mars. We went to the creek and caught tadpoles.

We were friends.

One day, while playing at my house, John's other friends were riding by on their bikes. They saw us playing and they rode up my driveway. I was excited, because I wanted to be their friend too. I wanted to be a part of this large group of friends who owned the neighborhood, who played hide-and-seek together, who created most of the neighborhood fun. But it wasn't to be that day.

They rode up the driveway, got off their bikes, and then came over to us. They asked John, "Why are you playing with that freak?"

"He's my friend." John said.

"Yeah? Look at him! Look at that red hair. What kind of a freak is he? We'd rather be dead, than red." they said.

And then one of them picked up a rock and threw it at me. A major moment of peer pressure would soon face John. As they all began to pick up rocks and throw them at me, they looked to John to see what he would do. I was dodging rocks, crying my eyes out, and trying not to look like too much of a wuss.

John had to dodge a couple of rocks to get out of the way. And as he stood there, watching them hurt me; you could see the struggle that was going on inside of him. I was looking at him, wondering why he wasn't doing something to help me. And they were looking at him wondering why he wasn't throwing rocks with them, if he was a part of their group. He could see both of the looks on our faces. Finally, the voice of the group won out. And John picked up a stone and hurled it at me.

What hurt more than the stone was the fact that my friend had just forsaken me. I was an outsider. I was different.

On that day, all I knew was that it sucked to be alone and it sucked to be different. What neither I, nor John, or anyone of that group realized that day, is that spiritually, we're all redheads. We've all been forsaken at one time or another. We are all outcasts, standing upon the same unsure ground. Spiritually, those around us are picking up the rocks that condemn us of our sin ready to be hurled.

In the passage from the Gospel of John, Jesus reminded the group of people that day who were about to throw the stones at the woman who was caught having sex with a man other than her husband, is that they have all sinned. Each one of them deserved to have that group of people hurl rocks at them. Jesus, without using the direct words Paul used, said to that group of people, "Look, you dorks. You've all screwed up. You've all been where this woman is today. You all know what it feels like to be alone. You all know what it feels like to have done something about which you're ashamed. You stand upon the same ground as this woman. So, what gives you the right to judge her? You're no different than she is."

Have you ever felt different? Have you ever felt alone? Have you ever felt forsaken? My friend, spiritually, you're a redhead! You've stood in a crowd of people, willing to condemn you for your actions, which are no different than the very actions of the crowd. It's so much easier for us to point the finger at others, than to point it at ourselves. That's why we judge people. When we judge others for doing the very same things we've done, we avoid having to face our own guilt and shame.

As a part of this, we need to first realize the times when we've been at the center of the circle, and then we need to look at the times when we've stood as a part of the circle. When have you been judged or pushed to the fringes? When have you felt all alone? And now ask yourself: when have you judged or pushed someone else to the fringes? When you have made someone else feel alone?

We all stand on the same ground before Jesus. He, and only he, has the right to point a finger of blame at us.

But you know what? Even though he has the right, he does not choose to exercise it. Instead of a finger of blame, he opens both his hands to us to show the scars of Grace.

May we learn to do the same.

I did not yet understand the full nature of Grace that day. The group left, but John stayed behind. And I pounded the tar out of him. It's interesting, somehow that made me okay in the eyes of the group. After that day, I was a friend to everyone. I had to resort to their ways to be accepted.

May I never do the same again.

I would rather be red, than dead. Spiritually red, that is...a reminder of the blood that flowed from Jesus' hands, purchasing Grace for all of us outcasts...all of us spiritual redheads.

THE THRONE OF GOD

Revelation 22:1

*P*alm Sunday is the day we celebrate in the life of the church when Jesus returned to Jerusalem. It's often referred to as his "triumphal entry," or his "victorious entry." All the people of the town lined the parade route that day. I imagine there were salesmen, hawking their wares. Items of food were being sold. Maybe they were even selling the very palm branches that were used to usher in the King?

I can imagine parents trying to corral their riled up children. I can imagine people setting out straw mats instead of aluminum folding lawn chairs on which to sit, to save their places right along the street. Oh and watch out! Don't you dare move their mats one inch! Their seats along the parade route are saved! It's a rule. Parents are corralling children, giving them little bites of parade-route goodies to feed their excitable souls and keep them occupied until the start of the parade. The pickpockets are out. Hey, wherever there's a good crowd of people, there's money to be made.

I wonder what the powers-that-be were thinking that day? "Who is this King?" they would ask with disdain. "Yes, we shall see...we shall see. And when we do, this upstart had better watch out. We will see who holds the real power." Little did they know.

As this is all going on, there is a scene just outside of town. Jesus has sent a couple of his buddies to go and fetch a foal of a donkey. Not even a grown donkey, mind you...a foal! There is no marching band. There aren't any visiting celebrities or dignitaries riding in convertibles. There is no parade-route manager with a clipboard, walking up and down the lineup, making sure all of the floats are in place. There is just a humble Jesus, and his ragtag group of friends.

The anticipation was building. People were not only excited because a parade was breaking up the routine of their lives. But they were also excited because they believed that finally, God had sent them a King to rule over them. A King of the Jews. A Messiah. A Savior.

People filled the streets to see the coming of this King. In their minds, they saw a majestic man, in flowing robes, coming down the street in a chariot of gold to return to a magnificent jewel-encrusted throne.

That's not what they got.

Imagine their surprise when they saw Jesus on the foal of a donkey. Imagine their surprise when they saw this lithe, lean Man, muscular from many hours of carpentry work, coming down the street with no armed escort, but instead, his disciples.

There is a word we shout each Palm Sunday. It's the word "Hosanna!" Yes, the exclamation point is needed here to help convey the passion of the word. It was shouted that day along that unlikely parade-route. But I have to wonder if it was shouted at first. As the tension in the air built to a feverish hum, the silence straining forth from expectant onlookers, the one exhibit, if we can call it that, rounded the corner and started to come down the street.

Nervous whispers.

"What? You've got to be kidding." a person asks the guy next to him.

"Is this it?" asks another.

"How can this man, riding on a foal of a donkey be our King?" asks a woman, despair hanging on the edges of her words.

But then it happens. *Jesus* happens. As he begins down the parade route, some begin to notice his serenity. They begin to sense the terrible power that lies within this peaceful man. They feel his authority emanating from him as he passes.

And so one bold person, rather hesitantly and haltingly, somewhat quietly, and yet hopefully shouts: "*Hosanna...*" People nervously look around at each other, seeking the approval of their neighbors, finding the same questioning looks on their faces. Someone else shouts the word again: "*Hosanna.*" This time, it's more forceful...more expectant. And then, like two drops of rain, birthing a flash flood, the parade comes into its own. Palm branches are waved. Tears flow from hopeful eyes as all the people gathered there that day shout from their hearts: "Hosanna!"

For you see, my friend, *Hosanna* means: "God save us!"

That day, Jesus, the King of all Kings, entered Jerusalem. But it took him almost a week to get to his throne. What throne? You ask. On Good Friday, we celebrate the enthronement of the King of Glory. Jesus went to the cross, his throne, willingly as good kings do. He went there knowing the weight of the crown he would bear. He went there knowing the consequence of the responsibilities he would carry. He wore the mantle of his own blood, the crown made of thorns. He carried the scepter of the spike pounded through his flesh. And he was enthroned upon a piece of carpentry that he never would have made in his profession as a carpenter.

And yet he did make that cross. Jesus is one with the Father. Jesus made the foundations of the earth, the earth itself, and everything upon it. He is the reigning King of Glory. He is the Alpha and the Omega, the Beginning and the End, in him and through him all things were made... even the cross.

This King, this glorious crucified King crafted his own throne with his gentle, calloused hands. There is majesty in this, although not in the way we think of the majesty of most kings. There is glory in the throne of the cross. But it is much different than the royal glory of which we think.

The majesty and glory of King Jesus and his throne come from the heart of a Servant-God.

Today, wherever you are, consider kneeling at the foot of the throne of Jesus. Place your life before your king as an offering to him. As you kneel, remember that the throne upon which Jesus sits exists because of his Love for us. From this throne, the scripture says, the Water-of-Life River flows. Eternal life flows from the throne of Jesus, from his cross where he bears the responsibilities of his Kingship: the sins of the world. Kneel before the throne, today, the cross of Jesus, and commit your entire life to him, to praising and worshiping this glorious King who shatters all of our notions about what true glory is.

Hosanna! Hosanna to the King of Kings!

WAKE UP!

For Maundy Thursday (the Thursday before Good Friday)
Mark 14:32-42

Maundy Thursday is weird to say. Maundy comes from the Latin *mandatum*. It's where we get the word: mandate, or command. And at the last meal Jesus shared with his best friends, he gave them one last mandate, or command. His command was simple: *Love one another.*

And so often, we fall asleep at the wheel of Life and forget the mandate.

I've done the same. I've fallen asleep at crucial times in my life as well. I can remember several times when I've been rudely awakened by a honking horn as I've swerved into someone else's lane because slumber came upon me unbidden. And as they rudely gesture to me, the translation is clear: "How can you sleep at a time like this?"

Jesus leads his disciples, truly his friends to a garden so they can pray together. He leaves the majority of the disciples together in a group, and then he takes Peter, James, and John along a bit further. Now, I can maybe understand the other disciples falling asleep. Maybe. They're obviously not the leaders. Their responsibility—or maybe their understanding of what Jesus is all about and who he really is, compared to Peter, James, and John—is rather shallow. They don't really get it.

Then again, maybe they do? Maybe it's Peter, James and John who don't really get it? Maybe Jesus knew that the others knew his true nature and so trusting in their faith, he left them alone. He figured they'd be all right. He figured they would stand watch with him. They would uplift him in prayer. They would stand firm.

Jesus told the disciples to sit for a while so he could go off to pray. What thoughts went through their heads that night? What did they think? Were they just befuddled about this mysterious supper they had together? Were they missing their families? Did they resent Jesus at all for what he had put them through? Do you suppose any of them complained? "Man this ground's hard. After that weird dinner, a nice warm bed would be great. What's Jesus up to? Why are we here? And why do the other three get to go with Jesus? Why do we always have to be the ones to stay back? When will we get our turn? How much longer will we have to stay? Man, did I tell you how uncomfortable this ground is?"

And then Peter, James and John...what were they thinking that night? Jesus leads them a bit further into the garden and then tells them, "I feel bad enough right now to die. Stay here and keep vigil with me." Do you think they had any clue how profound this statement was? The Lord...the Almighty Creator of the Universe itself...has just told them he feels bad enough to die. God himself, felt bad enough to die. Heartbreak.

Have you ever felt that way...bad enough to die? God has. Jesus, one with God the Father, came to a point that night of complete and total empathy for humankind. Lately there's a popular phrase that people say to others who are in a tough spot in life: "It sucks to be you." Do you suppose Jesus—God—thought something like this at that moment? "Wow. I can't believe how badly this hurts. It's really hard to be human, isn't it?"

Yeah. It is, God.

Sometimes, it's really hard. It's hard to feel all alone. It's hard when your friends turn their backs on you. It's hard when the bills stack up and the funds are low. It's hard when your spouse won't talk to you. It's hard when work consumes your time and you don't have much left over at the end of the day. It's hard, God.

In the midst of this realization, Jesus kneels to pray. And in this moment, his humanity cries forth to his Father in Heaven: "Can't you do something about this? Can't you get me out of this mess, Father?"

It is said that night when Jesus prayed, he prayed so hard he sweat blood. Such was his anguish...such was the intensity of his prayer. We don't have the answer to his prayer recorded in Scripture, but we can infer it by what Jesus said next.

Jesus asks for a way out. And I imagine the Father said something like: "My Son, I Love you so very much. And it truly breaks my heart to see you hurting like this. But Son, We both know there is no other way. And we both know why this has to happen. Something has got to happen to get their attention. They're surely not figuring it out on their own. And someone has got to pay the price for their sins. Shall we let them continue to pay the price of their sins by surrendering eternity? Shall we let them continue in bondage? Shall we let them wander as lost sheep, blind to their salvation?"

Jesus bows his head. He knows the Father is right. And although we don't really know what the Father said to Jesus that night, we know what Jesus said next: "But please, not what I want—what do *you* want?" Jesus has acquiesced. He understands. He knows what must come next. His divinity and his humanity have been at war over whether or not to proceed to the cross. Divinity convinces humanity. And with a new resolve, Jesus rises to meet the faces of friends who've been in prayer with him.

"How can you sleep at a time like this?!" the cry bursts forth from the heart of Jesus. Frustration to the point of tears grips him. They rouse from their slumber, ashamed at their lack of resolve. They can't meet the eyes of the broken-hearted Savior. Jesus knows who will be the founder of his bride, the church. And so he speaks to Peter directly: "Wake up! Can't you just stay awake with me for even a little while? You're almost ready. But not yet. Peter, you are going to need to see and feel utter despair and shame before you will truly understand what I am doing. You will need to surrender all of your pride. Stay awake with me, my friend. Pray against the temptations you will face."

Jesus turns to walk away and pray some more. In his heart, he knows Peter will sleep again. He knows the denials that will come. He knows the cross to which he will be nailed.

He knows.

And yet he kneels again to pray the very same prayer. And when done, he rises again to find Peter and the rest sound asleep *again*. Did Jesus wake them right away? Or, like a Loving parent, did he watch them sleep for a bit. Did he caress Peter's cheek with the back of his hand...with a Father's Love? Did he weep over them? Did he bless them as they slept in the same way I sometimes do when I creep into my children's bedrooms at night? Did one last tear stream down his face as he shouted and woke them again?

He went away, yet again, and prayed some more. It doesn't say what he prayed this last time. Did he pray for strength? Did he pray for courage? Did his heart so break for humanity that he simply prayed for our forgiveness? Did he pray for the Roman soldiers who would nail him to the cross? Did he pray for his disciples, that they would carry his Message to the world...that they would endure his trial and have one small glimmer of hope in the midst of great despair? Did he pray for Pilate? Did he pray for Judas, his great friend who would be the one to give him his last kiss...the one that would point out Jesus to the guards?

But he comes back yet again to find them sleeping. And like I had no excuse for falling asleep at the wheel...the disciples had no excuse either. They should have stayed awake. But they didn't. They, like us, couldn't bear the weight of the sins of the world. Overcome with grief, exhaustion, and the overwhelming emotion of the evening, they lost consciousness, only to be roused by God himself in that garden.

But by the last time, it was too late. Judas had come with the guards.

On this Maundy Thursday, I invite you to ponder the times when you've been asleep to what Jesus is doing when you should be awake with him. In what areas of your life is Jesus asking you to be awake and prayerful, but instead, you're sound asleep? All too often, I'm asleep during the times when Jesus is doing something great. I sleep through a moment when Jesus wanted me to be with him.

And so Jesus' last commandment to his friends is even more profound in light of what would happen later that evening: "Love one another."

Let's help each other to wake from the slumber of a life of apathy. Let's spur each other on in Loving the least, the last, and the lost. Let's rouse each other and wake each other to a life of radical discipleship that never sleeps.

And let's also offer a hand of grace to each other when we find one another deep in slumber, missing the work of Jesus in this world.

Love one another. Encourage one another in faith and offer a hand of grace.

"This is my body, broken for you. This is the blood of the New Covenant for the forgiveness of your sins."

Now *that* is Love!

THE PATH OF THE CROSS

For Good Friday
John 19:30

*T*oday is Good Friday. And every year, a question comes to mind for me: what's so good about it? I follow the steps of Jesus that day and the evidence of goodness seems lacking. Nails, thorns, a rough-cut cross, a whip, taunts, injustice...where is the goodness? Can you understand this? Can you? I'm not sure I do.

What does it feel like to be whipped? I'm thinking the pain would be worse than any of us has known. Strips of leather, quite possibly with shards of glass or pottery or rock knotted into the ends swung through the air with brutal force against the bare skin of a person's back. Imagine someone smacking you on the back with their hand. Doesn't feel good, does it? Imagine those little strips of leather and broken shards shredding the skin of your back. And not just once, but again and again. Most people pass out from such pain. Some die.

But the pain didn't stop there. What does it feel like to have a crown fashioned from thorns forced over your brow? Try to imagine it. Close your eyes right where you are at this moment and try to feel the pain of inch-long thorns gouging into the thin layer of flesh surrounding your skull. You can feel blood trickling through your hair, down your forehead, the saltiness of its crimson flow stinging your eyes. Again, pain like you've never known.

But it didn't stop there either. Now imagine that you've been whipped, stripped, crowned, and beaten, and they thrust a cross upon you that probably weighs more than two hundred pounds. The wood is rough. It's not at all smooth and shiny like the crosses we wear around our necks. Splinters splay themselves out from every inch of the rude symbol of our sin cleansing. And exhausted already from the abuse you have endured; this monstrosity is thrust upon you, splinters digging into your already bloodied back. In and of itself, this would be more punishment than I can even imagine...than I can really comprehend. My brain doesn't even know what to do with this painful information...let alone that which comes next.

After you have stumbled and fallen several times, you feel a brief moment of relief as a man helps you carry your cross the rest of the way up that horrible hill. But all too quickly, the relief passes, and you're there. Once there, you lay your cross down. You are grabbed roughly. All throughout, you are being teased. You look around, and you see the faces of your closest friends in the crowd. Is there any hint of recognition in their eyes? Do they even still know you? If so, they do not act like it. There is nothing showing on their faces that they are...were...your best friends.

You are shaken from this moment by the rough, war-scarred hands of soldiers who thrust you onto your back...onto your cross. Again, the splinters do their work, tearing at the torn pieces of your bloodied flesh. One of your wrists is grabbed, thrust against the rough wood. You see the glint of metal as the hammer is raised, poised to pound the spike between the bones in your wrist...forcing them to bend wider to let the spike through to its home in the rough wood of the cross. A loud clink rings out. At this point, I wonder if there is still pain? I wonder if by this point, the pain center of your brain has stopped functioning? If there is mercy in this world...maybe. Likely not. It's likely that the worst is yet to come.

At least there is a significant gap between the bones in your wrist through which the spike may pass. But then you remember, that once your wrists have been affixed to the cross, your ankles come next. Your other wrist has been attached. Somehow, it wasn't as bad as the first. You knew the pain. But then you feel rough hands grab your ankles, overlap them and...

A cry escapes your lips ripping through the sounds of the taunts of the crowd, piercing the darkness of the sky.

Is this remotely what Jesus felt? Again I ask, where is the goodness in Good Friday? Why did this happen?

Why? I'm not sure I understand what the motivation was behind this?

The only way possible is when I think of my children. I would do anything for my children. If I knew that my children were headed to Hell, I would go anywhere, endure any pain...carry any cross and even be nailed to it so they would not have to endure that torturous eternity.

The Father saw his children and knew the Hell to which they were headed. And the heart of the Father broke for his children. And so the Father came to the earth as the Son to walk amongst his people...to know their pain...feel their loss...celebrate their joy...and then be nailed to a cross.

What is good about today? The Love of the father for his children. As you walk the path of the cross on Good Friday, remember the profound Love the Father has for you. Jesus, God's Son...who is one with the Father, walked that path that day, enduring the unimaginable pain we have tried to imagine here, carrying his cross, getting nailed to it...because of the Love of the Father. For a brief moment, his humanity cried out. But his divinity remembered its purpose: to save his children.

Through the cross...the rough-cut splintery cross...your life has been spared. But now it's up to you...what's your choice? You are called to a choice today as you walk the path of the cross. Will you give your heart to the God who laid down his life for you? Will you Love him? Will you surrender all? Will you accept the sacrifice that has been made on your behalf? And will you take his Love with you and share it in this world?

Each one of us has known pain. One of the gifts of Good Friday is a God who knows pain. Jesus endured pain like most of us will never know, praise God. Through the path of the cross, not only do we receive the ultimate gift of salvation. But we also receive the empathy of Jesus—of God whenever we hurt and endure the unendurable.

As you contemplate your existence today, remember: the path of the cross has been walked for you by a God who Loves you.

WHICH THIEF WILL YOU BE?

Luke 23:36-46

As a child, he was not greatly Loved by his parents. His father was cruel and beat him regularly. He would lie in bed at night wondering why his father hated him. He would wonder why he didn't receive the same Love his friends did from their parents. He would wonder why the only attention he received was from his father's fists.

But then again, he would think, this attention was better than none. And so he discovered ways to get this sort of attention. He began to get into trouble at an early age. He began to hang out with those people...you know the ones. They're the ones you and I avoid when we're in public places. They're unsavory. We're not like those people...are we? I mean, look at how they dress! Look at the things they do! Can you believe them? These are the people at whom we sneer and turn up our noses.

These are exactly the sorts of people with whom he began to hang out. He would get together with them and get into all sorts of trouble. And while he was with them, he had to be tough. He began to build, brick by brick, a shell around his heart to protect it from ever feeling anything...especially while he was with his "friends." Because if they were to see any sort of weakness—and surely, his emotions were a weakness—they would capitalize on his weakness...exploit it...and then he would lose the only source of respect and belonging he had.

It feels good to be respected. It's wonderful to belong. Think of your sources of respect. Think of the groups to which you belong. How does it feel to be shown respect? How does it feel to belong?

Or maybe you don't receive respect...maybe you don't belong. Maybe you've been an outcast...a misfit...unLoved and unwanted? Maybe you don't get to play in all the reindeer games...in which case, you'll relate to this young man of whom we speak today.

As he grew, he sought his recognition from his "friends" by doing the things they challenged him to do. It started with small things, pilfering a loaf of bread or a small animal from a farmer. These were the things he did to gain acceptance from his "friends."

And the more things he did, the more respect they showed him. They challenged him constantly to do such things...they challenged him physically. And so he became more and more tough...able to beat up just about anyone. And as he became tougher, he also became more proficient at stealing. It became his craft at which he practiced. To compare him to other laborers, he would be considered a master in his craft. He was well respected in the thieves' guild. All knew of his thieving prowess. He was, by this time, seemingly untouchable.

Seemingly.

No one is invincible. No one is untouchable. This thief was hired by some wealthier members of society to steal from the temple coffers. He had the plan all worked out. He knew the different access points to the temple. He had researched the comings and goings of the priests and knew the ideal times at which to make his attempt. His plan was in place. The time set. The preparations made.

The night before his attempt, he lay in his bed, working through the plan one last time to make sure things would go off without a hitch. He discovered no glitches in his plan...except one. And it was a strange one...one he hadn't felt in a very long time. It was supplied to him from a quiet, almost inaudible voice from deep within—his conscience. "To steal from the temple coffers," it said, "wouldn't that be like stealing from God?"

He tossed and turned as he slept. He began to sweat. His sleep was fitful and rest-less. For even this hardened man, with a heart to match his calloused exterior...even this man believed in God.

He woke early, just before dawn, with a start. He sat straight up in bed...looking straight-ahead, chest heaving. He remembered his dreaming of the night before. He remembered the words from his conscience. And again, for the first time in a long time, he did something not familiar to him...he worried.

He sat there, embalmed in his worry—for God knows how long. And then, with a shake of his head, he roused himself from his worry and doubt. He crawled back into the shell of his hardened heart and re-donned his calloused exterior. He was tough. He was a master-thief. He could not be touched and there was nothing about which to worry.

He headed out from his abode to accomplish his task. He was prepared.

Sometimes we do things to self-destruct. Our subconscious gets in the way...or maybe it's our conscience... or maybe God? For the first time...maybe ever...he made a mistake. Everything had gone perfectly. His plan was masterful...but his hands were not. He dropped the container holding the temple offerings. Coins scattered everywhere on the floor. It made a noise that was easily audible throughout the temple. Priests came rushing in. Guards closed off exits.

He was caught. And as the guards closed in, he fell to his knees in defeat. There was no escape.

Being caught at what he did best...getting beat at your own game...this brings humility to one's life. As he knelt on the cold stone floor of the temple, he felt a burning inside him that he hadn't felt since he was a child. He tried to choke it back, but it remained...in fact, it spread. The stony shell of his heart cracked at that moment, and something Eternal found its way in. Would it be enough?

He stood trial. His sentence was passed. His reputation preceded him to the trial and his sentence was the maximum...death by crucifixion.

The date was set...it was to be the weekend of Passover.

He heard that there would be two others crucified that day as well. Huh...at least he wouldn't be alone. I mean, if he was going to go down, it wouldn't be alone. Right? Another heart attempt at shutting down from all emotion.

Crucifixion. "What a horrible way to die," he thought, "but think of the attention I'll get." For crucifixions brought everyone out. They were a major event. All would gather at the Hill Of The Skull for such an occasion.

Who can say exactly what happened that day. For truly, not much is recorded in Scripture of the goings on regarding our thief. But we do know this one thing: on that day, with nails piercing his flesh, he recognized his need for God.

What did it...or what will it take for you to recognize your need for God? For Love? Have you grown so full of yourself...or so hardened...that you're unable to admit that you need help? Have you been so wounded in life that you've closed down to all emotion because it just hurts too much to feel? Or have you become so self-reliant that you're unable to rely on anything or anyone outside yourself?

At points in my life, I most certainly have. And it's a terrible place to live. And it's lonely too. Thankfully, it didn't take physical nails piercing my flesh for me to be able to cry out to God.

But I can tell you, what it took hurt just as badly. To admit one's own shortcomings...one's failures...one's hurts...and yes, one's sins...this pain pierces to the depths of your heart...yes, to the core of your soul.

Take a look at yourself in the mirror today. What are your shortcomings? What are your failures? What are the wounds that hurt you? What are your sins? Recount them. Say them out loud. Write them.

Now, can you honestly say you don't need help? Can you honestly say, that in the face of these things, you can deal with all of them on your own? Can you honestly say you don't need Love?

Our thief could not. For that day upon the cross, he found himself in dire need of Love. And his heart, with years of disuse and misuse, found itself broken. Tears streamed down his face. And while one thief scoffed, this thief defended. While one thief rode his hardened heart to Hell, the other let his heart break and for the first time, he found his strength in what, for so many years, he thought of as weakness.

Will you let your heart break today? Will you take the risk of feeling? Will you open up and admit your need?

God chose to be crucified between two common thieves...to be associated with them. And we're really not all that different from them if we're honest. We've fallen short. We've screwed up. We've done things of which we're not proud.

But in the end, the choice is ours.

Which thief will you be?

THE FISH TENT

2 Corinthians 2:14-16

*M*any Point Boy Scout Reservation in the summer of 1981 became a place of legend for us. It is where a young man named Ted got his nickname "Cornbread." It is also where the Great Stone War of '81 took place. It is the sight of the Great AM Frog Migration. And it is also the origin of the Fish Tent.

We were mostly between the ages of ten and fifteen. Young, hormonally charged men, entrusted with pocket-knives, tents, and far too much free time. Too much free time equals certain trouble. Shades of *Stand By Me, Lord of the Flies*, and *Bloodsport*. Some of the things we did would most certainly frighten hardened members of both the Hell's Angels and the CIA.

We were a menagerie of humanity. There was Ja-hack and Dar-boy, Klingon and Bobbin-Swabbin, Venison and Cornbread, and oh, yes, there was young Richard. (Some nicknames just aren't re-printable)

Now, Richard has a bit of an interesting history. From an early age, he believed he was the "law" around the neighborhood and in our Boy Scout Troop. Most troops have patrol leaders, chaplains, and senior patrol leaders. Ah, but ours came complete with an MP: Richard. And let's just say that Richard wasn't the ripest apple on the tree at that point in his young life.

We mostly let him have his illusion of authority. It was just too much fun to watch, I guess. Imagine going down a path in the woods, coming up to some other Boy Scouts in camp, and then Richard goes into action. "Yeah, uh, did you know that your patch violates the Sewing Codes? The stitches used aren't up to code. I'm sorry young man, but I'm going to have to report you."

No, I'm not kidding.

This was our Richard. One fine day at Many Point Scout Reservation, Richard decided to get away from the madness of camp life and go fishing for a while. And I must tell you; he was, despite all odds, rather successful in his excursion. He came back with a stringer full of sunnies and crappies. Do you remember that part about Richard not being the ripest apple? This would be foreshadowing.

Richard, very proud of course, comes swaggering back into camp with his fish. He's thinking, "Hey, I've caught dinner for our camp." And I must admit, I was thinking that some fried fish would be a good deal after some of the meals we had been forced to consume. But in the midst of all this, something happened which forced Richard to have to store the fish and we all left camp.

We were probably off to some cool activity like sailing or *Capture the Flag*. Richard looked around for a place to store the fish. The coolers were full. We were staying in tents and so we had no electrical appliances that would keep the fish. Richard figured that he should at least get the fish out of the sunlight. Not bad thinking on his part, but not genius level either. Far from it.

Richard lifted up the back corner of his tent and placed the fish there.

It's amazing how quickly an 11-year-old forgets things. By the end of our activity, Richard had no recollection of having ever gone fishing that day. In fact, we all came back to camp, ate dinner, went to our evening campfire, and then headed off to bed with nary a thought of a certain stringer full of sunnies and crappies.

In fact, we didn't think of it for another three days. That's about the time the stench got so bad that people would actually gag as they walked past Richard's tent. In fact, it got so bad that our Scout Master could smell it in the next campsite and he came to investigate.

It wasn't a long investigation. All he had to do was follow the stench directly to the rotting, maggot-ridden fish corpses under the back corner of that poor Eureka tent. He lifted the corner and several young men heaved that day.

Paul, in his second letter to the church he helped start in Corinth, says that when we live lives of Love, we give off a sweet smell. It reminds me of the angel Michael in the movie of the same name. John Travolta plays an angel and wherever he goes, he gives off the smell of cookies. With Love in our lives, we give off a sweet smell. But here's the thing: only others who have Love in their lives and God Himself recognize the scent as sweet.

For all of those who do not know Love, we smell like rotting corpses. We are repulsive.

We cause heaving.

Those who are far from God's heart cannot recognize the true nature of our scent. Because our scent goes through the filter of their lives. Their lives are filled with the stench of brokenness. And so our sweet smell is filtered through the stench and comes out smelling rotten. Our scent is so different than what they're used to, that it can only be recognized as stench, rather than the perfume it really is.

Somehow, we have to find a neutralizer. We need sort of a spiritual version of Febreeze. We spray it on ourselves as we head off to share Love in this world. Instead of smelling the stench, they simply smell nothing right away. Thus we get the chance to share Love with them.

My friends, I think we do this by no longer being judgmental, and leaving behind self-righteousness. We dismount our high horses and walk right up to these people and say: "You know what? I'm doing my best at this. I'm tryin' to live a good life. But guess what? I am a hypocrite and I suck at this sometimes."

And for a brief moment, they get a waft of the sweet smell of Love on us. And it opens up some possibilities that didn't exist before. Suddenly they see God as not being the source of judgment and hypocrisy, but rather as a source of Love and forgiveness. And maybe it doesn't happen then and there, but now the possibility exists that at some point they will smell the sweet scent of Love and desire it for themselves and they'll want to change, leaving behind brokenness. And as it happens more and more, they'll begin to take on the sweet scent themselves. They will embark upon a new road. And they will repulse those on the road to destruction. Those who once could only detect our scent as stench have now become the stinky ones.

The beauty of this is, hopefully they remember what it was like to smell the stench of those who share Love in this world and can relate to those who can only smell Love as a stench.

While there is a way to neutralize our stench as Christians by leaving behind being judgmental and admitting our hypocrisy, there was no way to eliminate the stench of the Fish Tent.

Forever after that camp, no one wanted to get stuck with the Fish Tent. The Fish Tent, if it still exists, would certainly still carry the vestiges of its stench today. Too bad we didn't have *Febreeze* back then.

God bless you, Richard.

STAY AWAY FROM PUKE

2 Peter 2:20-22

Of all the disciples, I have always liked Peter the best. I like his boldness. I like his daring. And I can relate to his denial of Jesus. Peter is so real to me. Peter is not a holier-than-thou, high-and-mighty kind of a guy. He's salt of the earth, blue collar, blood, sweat, and spit.

Peter was the first out of the boat to walk on the water to Jesus. And then soon after, he denied his Friend and Savior three times in public.

Peter knows what it is to backslide, because he has slid backwards himself. He has had the faith to stand on the sea one moment, and then deny the very God who gave him such power the next. It is from experience that Peter speaks the words in our Scripture for today.

He's been there, done that, bought the t-shirt, and is now using it as a dust-rag.

Peter, remember he was first called Simon, was a fisherman by trade. He's been out to sea. He's caught fish. Peter probably had very rough, calloused hands and dark, leathery, weatherworn skin. His cheeks were ruddy from the winds blowing across the sea. His hair was probably lighter than many others from the many hours in the sun. Peter was an experienced fisherman. Peter has smelled rotten fish and seen men lose their lunches their first time on a boat.

Peter knows the stench and wretched nature of vomit. There's no doubt about it: vomit is gross. When we eat food, there is an undulating motion that our stomach and intestines uses to move food through our system called peristalsis. When we consume something that does not agree with us, which our body rejects as either foreign or poisonous, then the body puts that undulating motion into reverse. Reverse peristalsis...get this junk outta here!

When we experience Love, we go through a spiritual reverse peristalsis. All of the things in our lives that God views as either foreign or poisonous to us must be rejected. We must vomit from the depths of our souls, all those things that are not Loving.

Remember, Peter understands backsliding. And so he writes this to remind us of how terrible, how disgusting it is to return to our old way of life. He says it's like a dog returning to its vomit. And if you've ever had a dog, you know what they do when they return...they consume it.

The imagery of this is sick...disgusting...vile. I imagine that you're feeling a bit queasy right now. Good. Because this is exactly how we should feel when we think about returning to an un-Loving life. We should feel sick, disgusted, and vile.

Contemplate your old way of life before you knew Love. Remember how you lived, what you thought about, what you filled your head with, how you used the hours of your existence. And now contemplate returning to that way of life. And now, lest you be tempted to return, consider the image of ingesting the product of reverse peristalsis.

Peter likes to tell it like it is. He probably didn't use pretty words like vomit and reverse peristalsis. He probably just said the equivalent in their day of puke.

So, here it is in Peter-speak: if you return to a life without Love, it'll be like you're eating your puke.

It is on the faith of such a man, that God decided to build the Christian Church.

I Love Peter...and I Love the God who would pick such a man!

He Offers Us Diamonds

2 Corinthians 5:5

Like most days, you rise from slumber to face the dreariness of the day that awaits. While skies aren't always grey, that does not matter, for your soul is. You have succumbed to the monotony that is your life. You have surrendered your desires...your passions. The Dream Stealers have paid you a visit that has left you bereft. And so it is thus that you enter into your day, plodding through your existence.

As you trudge off into your day, you can do no more than lift one foot at a time, taking one step at a time, to think further than that would only increase the weariness of your soul. For the hopelessness of each step is almost too much to bear. And to think of one more step beyond this one that you now take would cause your will to crumble like dried clay.

Surely everyone must feel this way, you rationalize. Surely everyone has the same troubles, the same trials, and the same tribulations. Or maybe you think, "It's only me. I'm crazy." And so you convince yourself that life is not as bad as it seems. You paste a false smile on your face. You prop up your chin by force of will. You tell yourself that things really aren't all that bad. You carry a picture of a rainbow in your pocket that a child has colored as a symbol...a sign maybe, that there is Something more than this. The picture is tattered and worn around the edges.

The colors are faded, for you have spent many hours sitting outside gazing at this picture, futilely willing the dream into reality. When you gather with friends, you notice they have similar pictures. And you tell stories of better days and happier times as if they really happened. The gathered group's consciousness has a way of convincing even the most hopeless, if just for a moment, that Something Better Than This is out there.

Everywhere you go, you look for a glimpse of whatever that something might be. You search it out in everything. When you eat, you eat as if there will be no food for tomorrow. You wolf down every bite without even taking time to savor the taste. You seek out more food and better food and exotic food in the never-ending search for *Whatever That Something Might Be.*

As you walk through your life, you seek glances from others who seek the same. You search for a glimpse of Whatever That Something Might Be. You search for it in the beauty of others. You see someone whom you find attractive and at the edges of your vision, you think that maybe this is *Whatever That Something Might Be.* And so you strike up a conversation with this fellow seeker. And maybe in the intimacy of the moment, you sense the futility of searching for your answer here. Or maybe in the intimacy of the moment, your search goes too far. Instead of beauty, you find shame in each other's embrace. Your search for *Whatever That Something Might Be* has led you from bleak grey to cloudy black of night.

Your search continues, but it has gone from an idle curiosity to a fevered frantic scrambling for something onto which to grasp. Your gaze peruses television, movies, and advertisements. You search in games of chance...flipping coins from the bank of your soul. You survey images of lewdness and desire, because at least in moments like these, you've caught a glimpse of something transcendent. You've felt for a moment...a fleeting glimpse of something otherworldly. An echo of *Whatever That Something Might Be* seems to bounce off the clouds that envelop you.

And there is pain and loneliness. In this never-quenching search, you always seem to come up short. Your search dead-ends in brick walls of guilt, betrayal, loneliness, shame, and nerve-searing hurt. No matter where you seem to look, you are only able to catch the streaking trail of *Whatever That Something Might Be* as it flits further and further from you. And so you try to numb the painful advances on your soul with substances and solutions. You drink and smoke and consume things that seem to assuage the hurts. But the relief is so tempo-rary. You seem to plummet further into oblivion...

Until one day.

On one particular day, that started off no differently than the rest, full of its futility and half-hearted efforts, you were walking along and you overheard a conversation.

"My friend told me that he saw a City of Diamonds," said one man.

"Right." says another. "And my grandmother is the queen."

"No, I'm serious. I trust this guy like my brother. He was on a trip, came over the top of a ridge and right there, glinting with unimaginable exquisite beauty, stood a City of Diamonds with spires reaching into the Heavens." says the first man.

"Really?" says the other man, not daring to let himself hope. "I...I don't know..."

"I don't know either, but it's got to be better than this...I mean, it can't be any worse, can it?"

And off the two go. They head off into the day, down trails unknown to visit this City Of Diamonds. You stand there, wondering if it could be true. You wonder if you dare unleash the hope that you have pressed into the furthest recesses of your heart. You wonder if it's okay to un-cage the desire that is there. You take one step in the direction they have gone. And then another. Pretty soon, you've dropped your burden and you are running to catch up. You race down the path, sweat beading upon your brow, forming on your back, beginning to trail downwards. With wild abandon, you let go of all your pain, all your sorrow, and something that you've not dared to do in so very long bursts forth from your heart.

Against all your good sense, you dare to hope.

Something soars within your heart. It is wild and untamed. It is desire. It is passion. And within it, you see for the first time in a long time, a glimpse of the Dream. Tears stream down your face. Laughter exalts from your soul. There is no form to your running...no plan for your pace. You simply race faster and faster toward the horizon, toward the City of Diamonds.

As you come to the top of the ridge, you pause. You skid to a stop, steps fumbling, arms flailing. Your heart throbs within your chest. The salt from your tears is already drying upon your cheeks, causing them to feel taut. And as you timidly take the last steps to the top of the ridge, you are suddenly blinded with the brilliance of Diamonds. A feeling like you've never felt...like you've not even imagined in your dreams overcomes you. You fall to your knees, basking in the dancing beams of light, reflecting from the spires of the City. A cry of exaltation...of elation...of purest joy escapes your lips un-halted by any rationality.

And as you stand to resume your trek, you realize that the two men whom you have followed are already returning from the City. In their hands, you see the glimmer of diamonds.

With joy, they come running up to you to show off their diamonds. And just as they reach you, one of them trips, landing face first on the path before you. His diamond scatters from his hand and hits a rock, smashing it to splinters. A scream utters forth from him. "No!"

He rises to his hands and knees and begins to scoop up a handful of earth, glittering with splinters of glass. He sobs now. Despair has returned. The other man drops his piece of glass and it shatters as well. He helps his friend to his feet and they trudge off towards home. You consider doing the same.

But *Whatever That Something Might Be* will not let you.

You are not running anymore. Instead, only taking each step for the step that it is. You are deliberate. You take nothing for granted. You have no assumptions. All that is left is the hope that the brilliance of Diamonds glinting off the spires of the City is for real.

As you near the City gates, you notice a roadside stand just outside the gates. It has brilliantly colored banners waving in the breeze. And there is a sign which reads: "Diamonds For Sale $100." There is a line of would-be possessors, waiting to pay the price for one small "diamond." To their right, you see a small sign posted next to the City gates. It reads simply: "Surrender all and enter."

You stand as if a mule between two haystacks trying to decide. $100 seems like a pittance compared to surrendering all. As you stand there, the line at the stand begins to dwindle. One brave soul enters the City gates. The moment of decision is upon you now as you realize that there is no line for either the roadside stand or for the City gates. You must choose.

It is then that you notice the quotation marks around the word "Diamonds." And you remember the two wayfarers whose "diamonds" smashed upon the rocks much as their hopes did upon false assumptions. The glimmer of Whatever That Something Might Be flickers across your heart as your hand grasps the handle on the gate to the City.

You open the gate, step through hearing it slam forcefully behind you, locking out the despair of the drab dreariness that was your life. And as you enter, you are overcome with the brilliance of the City before you. It's brightness and beauty seem to be too much, and yet there is no pain.

And walking towards you is a man with extraordinary features. Fierce gentleness emanates from him. He walks to you...no, he runs to you, as if dancing his steps. He comes to you face to face, not uttering a word...not needing to. And he opens his hands to reveal Your Diamond. He speaks its name to you: Love. He speaks his name to you: God-with-us...*Love* with us.

And in this moment you realize that he is Whatever That Something Might Be. He and this Diamond are of the same substance. Unspeakable joy bursts forth from your being and can only be uttered in song and dance. Extravagant exaltation of your soul dances the Song that has always been there, but has gone un-uttered for it was squelched along with hope.

You rise and embrace Love. And as he breaks the embrace, he smiles that exuberant smile and he points. You know that he asks you to go forth with your Diamond to tell others. You know that many will not believe you.

You understand that many will be waylaid by the roadside stand offering dime-store imitations. You realize the folly of so many years of your life. And your heart goes out to the suckers who were taken in by the roadside stand offering glass imitations with all of the sparkle, and none of the Truth.

He offers us diamonds. Yet all too often we settle for glass.

PIECES OF GLASS

He offers us diamonds,
We settle for glass.
We see them so dimly
And so we pass by.
The treasures of God
are more than we dream.
He offers us diamonds,
Oh, why can't we see.

—Shane Burton © 2000

HE PADDLES ALONGSIDE US

2 Corinthians 1:3-5

I was in sixth grade when my friend and I were entrusted with a paddle, a canoe, and our belongings. With little training (one hour at Crooked Lake, a small lake in Coon Rapids, Minnesota), we were set afloat in the current of the Kettle River. We were less than novice canoers. Is there a level lower than this? How about greenhorn or tenderfoot canoers. Skill? We had none. Fear? We had much! Experience? One hour on a lake.

Did you know that canoeing on a lake is radically different than canoeing in a river? We didn't. We figured that canoeing was canoeing no matter where you did it. We couldn't have been more wrong about this. Also, did you know that there is a class system for rivers? Apparently some rivers feel they're better than others and so they've assigned themselves classes to differentiate between upper- and lower-class rivers.

For example, the Mighty Mississippi is mostly a class 1 river. It's lazy; it winds about, meandering through the countryside. Then you have a river like the Colorado River that is often a class 5 river. Major whitewater and rapids. Prepare for certain death unless you're well trained or with a guide. Novice is not a word you want to hear in conjunction with a class 5 river. Novice = death.

The Kettle River, depending upon the level of the water, ranged from class 1 to class 4, depending upon where you were and when you were. Well, dear friends, we were there in the middle of the scorching summer heat. Water level is low. Rocks are exposed. Current is swift. And 6th graders are clueless and petrified.

We also thought that it would be a good idea to pick the coolest canoe we could find. We didn't want any of the boring aluminum canoes. Certainly not! Especially when there was a cool fiberglass canoe that was a replica of an old Native American canoe, complete with the high bow and stern.

Here's a question for you nautical types: what happens when you combine wind with a large, flat surface area? That's right! You get a sail. And because of the high bow and stern on our canoe, we had a lot of surface area. So, when the wind kicked up, there was a problem.

I was in the canoe with my friend, Burt. As I said, we were hormonally challenged greenhorn canoers. We didn't know the difference between an oar and a paddle (look it up). We got into the river with our canoe without tipping it over. This was a feat in and of itself, considering we weren't thinking at all of canoeing. We were discussing the lasses from our classes. The day was sunny. Life was good. It was a Pez moment. We were doing just fine.

And then came the wind. You see, we didn't really understand the fine art of steering a canoe. Also, our scrawny twelve-year-old arms weren't able to push all that hard in the wind. We went from fine to "Oh dear God, somebody help us!" in a matter of minutes. We had no control over our canoe. We were spinning like maple tree helicopters as we went down the river. Older boys went by us laughing. We were beginning to get scared. And then we did get scared. We began to hear something. It sounded much like a train coming in the distance. White noise with some thunder mixed in.

It was the sound of river rapids approaching.

We began in the class 1 part of the river. We were rapidly approaching the class 4 parts. "Danger Will Robinson! Danger!" Traveling sideways rapidly approaching rapids is not a place you ever want to find yourself. We made it safely through the first fifty yards with just a few bumps and scrapes along the bottom of the canoe. However, the five-foot drop was yet to come. We were still headed sideways. Large rocks are everywhere. Water is coursing through the rock maze, sloshing about in a wild thunderous fray. Our canoe turned slightly so we were at least going diagonally and we hit a monster rock. The speed of the current propelled us on top of the rock. Our canoe was dangerously close to tipping over and we were absolutely stuck. Our scrawny arms weren't able to do a thing. We used our paddles to try and push us off the rock, but it was no good.

And then we saw him, our old Scoutmaster, Don McGrath. Very calmly he paddled through the wild current. His face was calm. There was even a hint of a smile there. Burt and I looked at each other and realized neither of us had breathed in a while and when we saw his face, our breathing began again. Don canoed right up alongside us. He then attached his canoe to ours and jumped out of his canoe into the raging torrent of the Kettle River. Sacrificing his safety for ours, he pushed us off the rock and then, while traveling through the rapids still, he was able to climb back into his canoe and tow us to safety. Don then had us separate and we split up and went with other people in their canoes for the rest of the trip.

Don came up alongside us and led us alongside others. Burt and I weren't able to really help anyone out in the canoeing area of life. But in other areas, we were there. I'd like to say that God used us mightily at that point to help others out. But that's just not the case. We were twelve, inexperienced, and rather selfish.

But this is exactly how God uses us in life. He comes up alongside us to rescue us. He did this through Jesus, who came right up alongside each and every one of us through his birth, his life, his death, and his resurrection, to rescue us from traveling sideways down the rapids of life. And then he led us to safety. And he led us alongside others who were also traveling sideways so that we could help them. God uses us to help one another. God uses us precisely because we have had hard times so we will be able to relate to others who are going through their own.

God uses broken people to reach broken people.

Because God knows what it's like to be broken. He was broken for each of us upon the cross by the nails of our collective sins.

Are you traveling sideways down the river of life? Pray for God to send someone to rescue you. Chances are, you'll find someone there for you who was just as lost at one point in their lives. They're just as broken, just as confused. But they've been there before and they are there for you now.

Right now, is your canoe pointed relatively downstream and you're doin' okay? Well my friend, pray for God to use you today. Pray for God to open your eyes to others downstream from you who are spinning out of control. Pray that God will use you, yes *you*, my friend, to paddle up alongside them to help them out.

It might be dangerous. It may require sacrifice. It may require pain.

But when you were lost and your canoe was spinning wildly out of control, wasn't it nice to have someone else risking his or her safety for yours? Didn't it feel good to be rescued? And in the moment, did you really consider the sacrifice that had been made on your behalf? It was dangerous for them. It required sacrifice. It may have even required pain. And yet someone was there for you. God brought them up alongside you.

It was dangerous for Jesus. It required the ultimate sacrifice. And it certainly required pain. God came up alongside us to rescue us from the raging torrent.

Today, he wants to use you to paddle up alongside someone else. In return for your sacrifice, you will receive the joy of having rescued someone. But you will also receive healing comfort promised in equal measure.

Scan the horizon of the part of the river of life you're traveling for people whose canoes are out of control. And remember the times when you've been in the same situation.

They are broken...just as you have been at times in your own life.

God uses broken people to reach broken people.

Keep your eyes peeled...and paddle!

Do You Get It?

John 13:2-8

*C*alculus was almost the death of me. I was in advanced mathematics courses all the way through middle school, junior high, and then into senior high. First there was algebra in 8th grade, geometry in 9th, higher algebra in 10th, elementary functions (trigonometry and pre-calculus) in 11th, and then, the crème de la crème of high school math: calculus.

Mr. Swenson was our teacher. And truly, he wasn't really a teacher. He was a purveyor of information. He was a college professor who would come to the slums...err ah, to our high school and teach one course. Just one. Calculus.

Ugh.

He would walk with the dignity of a British lord as he marched into our classroom. We met just a couple of times each week for one hour. He looked rather like Winston Churchill. Mr. Swenson was a bit pompous and aloof. To this day, I don't know if he came to our class to dispense mathematical wisdom from on high or to inflict great pain. Maybe it was a combination of the two. Out of a classroom of twenty-three teenagers, maybe two really wanted to be there. I'll bet you had them in some of your classes as well. They're the ones who actually could speak Klingon, knew the limitations of dilithium crystals, and could tell you the maximum velocity that could be reached on "impulse power."

They Loved math. And not only did they Love math, but they adored calculus.

And they got it.

I'll never forget that class. Because as each day in Mr. Swenson's class would go by, it seemed another person would get it. You could almost see the light bulb turning on over each person's head as they got it.

Sadly, not everyone did. I managed a passing grade. But the light bulb moment never came for me.

I didn't get it.

Over and over, the disciples of Jesus just don't get it. They're standing right next to the Savior of the Universe and they don't get it. Daily they're walking with the One who created the Universe and they don't get it.

They're with God. And they don't get it.

There are times when I read these passages and I think "duh!" How do you not see who this Man is? How do you not see Jesus for who he really is?

I think it has to do with the fact that maybe God wasn't done revealing who he is. There was more about himself that needed to be shown to the disciples so they could tell the world...so they would be motivated to tell the world and not just a few of their buddies. One of the final revelations to the disciples happens in this scene.

Jesus wants to show his disciples the true heart of his Father. He wants to show them his Servant heart. He wants to show them what true Godliness is.

Here, we see God as the Ultimate Servant.

In this scene, we see the Almighty God, humbling himself before his friends to serve them. The Omnipotent God sets aside the Majesty we think of when we think of God, and redefines the word. True majesty is to serve out of a heart of Love. But Peter doesn't want this. He doesn't want Jesus to serve him because he doesn't see himself as worthy. Because Peter, of all the disciples, was the one whom I think came the closest to getting it. He had a glimpse. Peter went to the mountaintop with Jesus and saw him shine with bright light. Peter walked on water with Jesus. Peter had an inkling of Jesus' divinity and thus felt unworthy to receive the gift of his service. But unless Peter experiences what it is like for God himself to serve him, he will never be a part of the great works of God. Because for God, it's all about a servant heart.

If you can right now, take off your shoes and socks and take a look at your feet. Feet are kind of weird. We keep them covered up all of the time. We hide our feet from the world. They're smelly. They're funny shaped. They're even kind of embarrassing. Most of us are pretty ticklish on the bottom of our lowest appendages. Feet seem sort of silly, and at the same time, there is an intimacy that is associated with our feet. I think this intimacy is part of the point. Because servanthood is intimate.

Now close your eyes and imagine Jesus kneeling in front of you. He kneels there all-mighty, all-knowing. As he kneels in front of you, he sees the depths of your heart in this moment. He knows with what you struggle today. He knows the burdens you have been carrying. He knows the sins you've tried to hide. He knows the shame you bear. He knows...and there he is, kneeling before you, this Almighty God, King of All Kings, Savior of the Universe— there he is, kneeling to serve you. He wants to wash your feet. How does it make you feel to know that God would kneel before you and wash your feet? Does it humble you? Does it shame you?

I must confess to feeling both of these. I feel humbled to know that God Loves me this much. But I also feel ashamed because I know that I have not knelt nearly enough at the feet of others to serve them. And in this, I deny the true nature of the Father.

This Servant knelt in the dust to wash your feet, and then rose and carried our sin and shame upon his cross. He made our feet clean to show us the heart of the Father. He made our hearts clean upon his cross so that we will one day see the Father face to face.

God was willing to kneel at the feet of his children to teach them to kneel before others. God was not just willing to do this...he had to, because, after all, that's who he is.

If the occasion were ever to arise, I would with all humility, kneel before Mr. Swenson and wash his feet. An unlikely event...to be sure. But wouldn't it be just like Jesus to make it come about? That'd be pretty cool.

God bless you, Mr. Swenson. I hope I have the opportunity to serve you someday.

THE GREAT BUBBLE BLOB

1 Corinthians 5:6-8

I had a friend in high school, for whom I often housesat. Admittedly, my motivations for housesitting were not entirely altruistic. How often does a 17- or 18-year-old guy get a house to himself for a week? On these occasions, whilst my friends were on vacation, I was at their house with a stack of videos (tons of "redemptive" violence, of course), bags of chips, cans of pop, and large pizzas and double-cheeseburgers all to myself. During their vacations, I would go on a marathon video-munchy-couch-potato-palooza. It was beautiful. I'm tearing up just thinking about it.

On one of these occasions, I figured I'd better get the dishes done before they got home so I began to load the dishwasher. A bit of history for you: growing up, I never had a dishwasher. We did our dishes by hand with Palmolive dish soap, a rag, and flour-sack towels to dry them when finished. Those of you overachievers who like to work ahead are probably beginning to put the pieces together already. I got all the dishes into the dishwasher, a feat in and of itself for an inexperienced, novice dishwasher operator like me. And then I looked underneath the kitchen sink for the box of powdered dishwasher soap. I grabbed the luminescent green box and heard the pitter-patter of about five granules of soap powder. Truly not enough to do the job.

I dug underneath their sink some more, thinking there might be some left in the back of the cupboard or something. But alas and forsooth, I found nothing. Well, nothing that is, except a bottle of Palmolive. Uh huh. Are you getting it yet?

Being a child of the 70s and 80s, I remembered clearly what happened on the one episode of the Brady Bunch when one of the boys was washing clothes and poured in an entire box of detergent. The washing machine came to life and began spewing forth prodigious amounts of suds. I had learned my lessons well from TV (Hey, it's where I learned math, grammar, science, and history you know! Do you remember *Schoolhouse Rock?*)

Don't put too much soap into the machine.

I also was aware of the concentrated nature of dish soap and so I figured that one drop ought to be just fine to put in the dishwasher. I turned the dishwasher on and just about then, my pizza arrived. I grabbed the pizza, popped in a movie, and sat down on the couch in my gluttonous reverie.

After about a half hour, I began to see movement out of the corner of my eye. At first, I ignored it, figuring I was just imagining things. After a few more minutes, I knew I was seeing something and so I turned to look...

And there, creeping around the corner, was a blob of suds, coming to get me. I yelled something profound like "Holy bubbles, Batman!" leapt from my perch on the couch and ran to the kitchen, sliding through the Great Bubble Blob. I quickly turned off the dishwasher and began to mop up the suds. And then I called for help. I called my mom.

"Mom!"

"What's wrong, Shane?" she asked, sounding concerned.

"Well, I ah...I goofed, mom." I said, kind of sheepishly.

"What happened?" she asked, being a cool mom.

"Um, it's like this...I...well...I put dish soap into the dishwasher..."

Before I could even finish, she yelled, "You what?!"

"I put dish soap into the dishwasher...but I only put in one drop."

"Shane. Well, I guess you learned better on that one! Here's what you need to do, empty the dishwasher and run it several times through with just cold water. That'll make the suds go away and you'll be fine."

"Thanks, Mom." I said.

"You're welcome. Good luck." she said.

Well, she was right. A couple of hours later, I had the mess all cleaned up. And when my friends returned home, they were none the wiser. But I told them anyway. I think I said something brilliant like, "Did you know you can get soap suds to shrink with cold water?"

If you put in the wrong soap, life can go seriously awry.

That's pretty much what Paul, the first-century church starter, was telling us in the fifth chapter of his first letter to the church in Corinth. "Hey folks, ya know what? If you keep pumping yourselves up, you're headed for a fall. Yes, it feels good to be Loved by God. Yes, it's wonderful that we're created in his image. It feels good to be noticed and recognized, doesn't it? But guess what? It ain't all about you. It's about Love. So, stop puttin' in that stuff that's going to puff up and make you appear larger or better than you are. And start only putting in what will make you to be the kind of loving person God has created you to be."

For me, it's sometimes just a matter of putting on some clothes, cologne, and a little extra gel in the hair and I'm puffing myself up to look better than I really am. Other times I'll exaggerate a story to make it look better. I get to thinking things like, "If only I drove a brand new, candy-apple red, 1969 Camero Z-28 with white racing stripes, then I'd be cool. Or if I only bought my entire wardrobe from Calvin Klein and Eddie Bauer, then I'd be all right. If only we ate at the right restaurants. If only I had enough money. If only I had a cool boat. If only I wore the right shoes. If only I had the right friends. If only...if only..."

And then God gently says, "If only you'd turn to me, dear one."

"What? Who's that?" I ask.

"You know Who I Am! Hello! Don't you remember calling out to me when that car almost smashed into you? Who do you think took care of that for you? If only you'd turn to me...if only you'd put me in your life first, then everything else will fall into place, as it should be. You won't need to build yourself up at all if you put me in first. Because I will build you up in a way which will astonish and amaze everyone. I will build you up to be the person I've created you to be. So, what's it going to be, Shane? Are you going to continue to put in all that other stuff so that you can feel better about yourself? Or are you going to turn to me?"

"Can I buy a vowel?" I ask.

God laughs and says, "Sure, you can buy an I."

"An I?" I ask.

"Yes," says God. "I Am."

"You are. You are. You are. YOU ARE!!!"

God turns to the archangel Michael and says, "Hey, Mikey! I think he likes it!"

"I think I get it now God. It ain't all about me...it's all about you."

"Ah, young grasshopper, now you're beginning to see." says God.

"God?"

"Yes, Shane."

"You get to be first in my life."

"About time." says God with a smile.

CROCODILES AND ELEVATORS

Romans 2:19-21

I went to a wedding a couple of years ago. Weddings are wonderful occasions where amateurs are thrust onto the stage of life, mostly unprepared. I secretly take a great amount of pleasure in some of the "surprises" which accompany these grand events. I've never seen a wedding go perfectly. Not one. There's always at least one speed bump...if not a sinkhole.

At this particular wedding, the "surprises" were at an all-time low. I kept waiting for the bride to hurl or a groomsman to split his pants. Just a couple of minor glitches that did nothing to overshadow the grandeur, Love, and faith of the wedding of my cousin and his Lovely bride. Both the mother of the bride and the mother of the groom cried happy tears; their respective spouses heaved deep sighs of relief, knowing that soon the insanity would cease.

I'm a lot more used to doing weddings than being a spectator. And at this one, I was unable to find a babysitter for my children. And so I dressed 'em up and brought 'em with. The eldest child was to my left. The youngest was to my right, in between her mother and I. And our middle child was on the far right. This worked for about half the service. And then the youngest got fussy.

Because it was my cousin's wedding, my ex-wife took our youngest out of the sanctuary, leaving me to enjoy the rest of the service. One boy on my left, one on my right. It worked pretty well for most of the time. A couple of times

I strenuously whispered "Will you sit still?" or "You just wait until we get out of here young man." But that was about it!

Meanwhile, my ex-wife and two-and-a-half-year-old daughter roamed the hallways of the church. The roaming was mostly a lot of running on the part of my daughter and a lot of chasing on the part of my ex-wife. They looked in rooms, perused bulletin boards, and watched a family of unicyclists practicing in the gymnasium.

During this roaming, my little girl kept asking my ex-wife where the crocodile was. Rather perplexed, my ex-wife had no idea where the crocodile in this church could be. Didn't know they had a pet. What does a church do with a crocodile? What could worship be like in such a church? Imagine it...

Having no idea where the crocodile was, and telling my daughter repeatedly that she was pretty sure there was no crocodile in this church, they kept roaming the hallways—vagabond wedding escapees. And as they walked down one hallway, Darby, my daughter, ran to the elevator and said very excitedly with that sort of a "Eureka, I've found it!" tone in her voice: "The crocodile!"

My ex-wife stood there, head cocked to one side, one eyebrow raised with that I'm-a-dog-and-you've-just-faked -the-throw look upon her face. And my very confused ex-wife said to Darby, "Honey, that's not a crocodile."

It was our daughter's turn to look confused. The gears in her little brain were grinding away furiously trying to figure out the quandary. The look on her face said, "If it's not a crocodile, then what is it?" And then an "Aha!" look came over her little face and she proclaimed question-ingly: "It's an alligator?!"

And then the "Aha!" look came over my ex-wife's face as she finally came to understand Darby's confusion. My ex-wife said to Darby: "It's not an alligator. It's an e-le-va-tor."

My little girl was sure she knew what she was talking about.

And so we all too often think the same. We strut about with smug looks on our faces thinking we've got it together. We think we have all the answers. We think we're pretty hot stuff.

I Love the author of the Scripture for today. His name is Paul. Paul was a bold, zealous man. He certainly wasn't afraid to speak his mind. And he most definitely wasn't afraid to call people out when he saw them screwing up. In this letter, he's writing to some people who think they've got it all together. Apparently they don't. The letter has 16 chapters!

Paul is giving the people of the church in Rome a little heads-up. He's reminding them that they're not half as cool as they think they are. A good reminder for us as well. Because truthfully, when I'm in worship on a Sunday morning, I have often thought to myself, "Huh...at least I'm not as bad off as they are." What arrogance! What pride! And from the pastor. Yuck! And that yuck is for me. For who am I to proclaim myself better than anyone?

Because just when we're sure that it's a crocodile. Then we're told it's not and so it must be an alligator, right? Ah...silly us. We ain't the sharpest tools in the shed, are we? Come on, admit it. Hey you there, with the IQ of 148, get over yourself! It's not a crocodile, nor is it an alligator. We've been completely mistaken.

Paul's point? "Look out for each other. Don't pretend that you've got it all together...because the only One who does is God and guess what...you're not God! Help each other to know what's a crocodile, what's an alligator, and what you're just plain ol' confused about. Don't be so arrogant to think that you've got it all together. Turn together to the One who does...Jesus Christ."

Darby now knows what an elevator is. Now if I could only get her to stop calling her brother her "favorite cow-pie poke"...ah, but that's another story.

GETTING AWAY WITH IT

John 6:70-71

When you were in school, did you ever do something to get yourself in trouble, but didn't get caught? I remember one time in 6th grade, in Mrs. Satre's class. This girl and I had a spitball fight. A big one. In fact, we were chewing up entire pieces of notebook paper to throw at each other. Besides being pretty darn gross...it was also a lot of fun. It was fun until one of our shots went astray and Mrs. Satre finally noticed that something was going on.

"Okay. That's enough! I've had it up to here. (She never did indicate where "here" was) Who is throwing spitballs in my classroom?"

Everybody sat there silently.

"Who is the guilty party? Who made this mess? Tell me, who!?!?" Her ire was peaking.

And I sat there with a silent war raging in my head. "Should I admit it? Nah. She won't find out. But what if she already knows? Won't it be better for me if I just admit it? What's the right thing to do? Who cares?! She'll never find out. Nobody will talk...b..but what if they do? Then I'll really get it. Oh man...what should I do?"

At the time, we were greatly thankful that our classmates did not betray us. We all sat there silently, waiting for the storm to blow over. It did. Mrs. Satre went back to teaching us some other interesting fact about the English language.

I remember in that moment, that I did not feel smug. Actually, I felt guilty. I knew that everyone else around me knew who was throwing spitballs. And the one person who actually should have known didn't. I was afraid she'd find out. I was afraid she'd have some serious consequences for me. I was afraid and guilty.

I imagine that at that moment when Jesus said, "Still, one of you is a devil," that Judas was feeling similarly. I imagine that he was afraid. I imagine that he was feeling guilt. His situation, however, was a bit reversed from mine. In my situation, the whole class knew, but the teacher did not. In Judas' situation, the class did not know, but the Teacher did.

I wonder if Judas knew that Jesus knew. I imagine Judas sitting there imagining all sorts of scenarios and being filled with paranoia. I imagine the war that raged on inside his head as Jesus told them that one of them is a devil.

"I wonder if he knows it's me? What am I going to do? Okay, get a grip Judas. Hold it together. Just a little while longer and it's a done deal. But look at the way he's looking at me...he must know it's me. No, no...he couldn't. How could he? Breathe. Don't make eye contact again. Judas, all you're doing is telling them which one Jesus is so they get the right guy. It's not like you're killing him or anything. Hasn't he caused you enough trouble? Yeah, there's been trouble...but...well, I Love the guy. And...well...I don't know. I don't want to...but I have to."

I imagine that Judas has a heart. I imagine that Judas was ripped up inside about this. I imagine that Judas quickly wiped away a tear so that no one would see and suspect it was him. But I imagine the tear was there. And that it trickled slowly down his face as he looked into the eyes of his Savior. Because I also imagine that he knew...that he suspected...that his action...that simple kiss...would snowball into absolute betrayal.

Jesus looked out over his Twelve...his closest friends...his students and he knew that one of them would betray him. In fact, he knew which one. And here, he gives Judas a chance to 'fess up. But Judas doesn't take it. He lets it play through, just like I did in Mrs. Satre's classroom.

I got away with it.

So did Judas.

What have you gotten away with? What have you packed down deep inside the furthest recesses of your being that still gnaws at you? What are the things you've done that make you like Judas?

Every day, Jesus gives us a chance to 'fess up. Take him up on it. Tell him the things you've done which you've "gotten away with." Ask him for forgiveness. Take it a step further, call up the person and 'fess up. Apologize. Get things right between you...and between you and God.

Judas never did this. And his guilt consumed him to the point where he could take it no longer. He was so filled with shame, guilt, and pain that he took his own life.

I wish Judas had stuck around a little longer. Because then he'd know the rest of the story. He'd know about hope. He'd know about grace. He'd know that there's always a chance to 'fess up. He'd know the kind of Love that God has for him and that God's Love is bigger than all of our sins. God's Love is even bigger than betrayal. God's Love can take it.

Did Judas *really* get away with it?

Let's let God be the judge of that.

I should call Mrs. Satre.

Just Passin' Through

Hebrews 11: 13-16

My 13th great-grandfather was Stephen Hopkins. A fair amount is known about him as he helped to finance a little excursion across the Atlantic on a boat named the *Mayflower*. He was most definitely not a Puritan. In fact, from what I've learned, he actually set up some sort of a pub when he arrived in what would become the United States of America.

Imagine life four hundred years ago. Imagine the conditions in which people existed. Imagine the modes of transportation. Imagine bathing habits. Imagine what was eaten. Imagine their medical care. Seriously, spend some time calling to mind what each of these things was like.

There were no roads paved with tar. There were no planes, no cars, no motorcycles...there weren't even bicycles. If they had transportation, it was probably in the form of a horse or a boat. But most couldn't afford simple modes of transportation.

And what about their food? Homogenization was not in their vocabulary. Sterilization was not a common concept. They ate raw milk, eggs, and sometimes raw meat. And I'm guessing—it's just a guess, mind you—that the idea of antibacterial soap hadn't crossed their minds either. In fact, if you do some reading in this area, you will find that for some, the poorest servants, they were able to have one bath a year and one set of clothes per year...and they were sewn into them. Each spring, they were cut out of their clothes for bath time and then given their new set of clothes.

And medical care? *If* they had access to it, it was largely based on superstition. And the concept of anesthesia was not largely available, other than that which came in a whiskey bottle or a good whack to the head.

Those were the everyday living conditions. Now, imagine that someone has come through town saying that there is a new country across the ocean. It's a land where you will be free to practice your own religion. But you will have to give up everything you have to start over in this new land. And not only that, you will be out to sea for months in God-knows-what conditions, for the *chance* to live in this new land. Just for the chance...

I imagine that the new land sounds pretty good. I imagine the idea of starting over seems wonderful. But I can also hear the voice of practicality and reason saying: "Don't do it...you'll have to give up everything you've worked so hard for. Don't leave behind this sure thing."

The voice of adventure and hope responds: "But, think of what you will miss if you don't! Imagine worshiping God in the way you feel called! Imagine not living under direct rule of the monarchy! Imagine! See the vision of this new land and all that it holds for you! Imagine..."

There is a stirring in your spirit and you respond by raising your hands to the sky to ask God what he thinks about it. And you recall the story of Moses in the wilderness for forty years. You remember how he stood upon the banks of the Red Sea with the horde of Pharaoh at his back. And you remember how God opened the Sea and how God was faithful throughout the forty years. You remember the faith of Moses.

You decide to go.

You board a ship with your family and set out to sea, not knowing what lies in store for you. At first, the journey is a celebration of what you're leaving behind and of what is ahead. The mood is high. Morale is good. But then a storm hits, and some of your fellow passengers are lost over the rail. After more time has passed, several more die from illness. And pretty soon, the days begin to blend into each other in a never-ending haze of sunrise and sunset, each swell of each wave bringing another version of the sun before your eyes.

And soon, there are those among you who despair. They give up hope. No longer does the song of God's promise sing in their hearts. No longer do they see the vision of worshiping God freely in a new land. These people are homesick for the old country and they haven't even seen the new. No longer do they sense the presence of the Almighty God on your ship, which is named after a flower blooming in the springtime...a sign of hope. No longer do they have hope.

These people don't have the Promised Land in hand and are not able to continue believing in a far-off, unseen land of promise.

But not you. You know you worship a God who is bigger than this boat. You know your God is bigger than this sea...in fact, you know your God is Lord of this sea that you ride upon day in and day out. You know your God is the Lord over each sunrise and sunset and you know it is up to him each day whether the sun will indeed rise or set. It's God's choice every day. The sun does not have to rise...unless God feels like it. You know that your God has called you to this great adventure and will be faithful to you.

For you, you're just passin' through the Atlantic. You know something more awaits you.

And as day fades into day, and each wave seems like the last, you go along trusting in the promises of God: that you are Loved, that God goes with you no matter what, and that God is leading you onward in your life to something more.

And finally, one day as you awaken, you hear the sound of a bird. One simple squawk of a sea gull and the hope that has burned in your heart becomes an inferno of joy, because you know this simple bird is a sign that you are nearing land. God has led you to this new land. And you have trusted in his leading.

In this letter, Paul encourages us to hold onto to our faith in that which is not yet seen. Paul knows what it's like to be unable to see. Paul knows what it's like, because the very God he serves, is the God who blinded him with glory to get his attention. And during that time, Paul...or Saul as he was still called...had to trust that God had things under control...because he knew that he certainly did not.

Paul had the kind of faith that burned in the darkest nights. Paul had middle-of-the-storm faith. Paul had dark -night-of-the-soul faith. Paul had lost-all-your-money faith. Paul had lost-all-your-friends faith. Paul had throw-me-in-prison faith. Paul had *Jesus* faith.

Paul had faith in Jesus to lead him through the darkest night and the wildest storms. Paul had faith in Jesus to sustain him even though he lost everything and everyone. Paul had faith behind bars that was a witness to the very guards who held him captive.

And because of this kind of faith...because of his faith in Jesus...lives were changed...stuff happened...hearts opened for the Love of God.

How's your faith today? Do you have my-kids-are-screaming faith? Do you have my-car's-broken-down faith? Do you have lost-all-my-money faith? Do you have my-friends-have-abandoned-me faith? Do you have Jesus faith?

Do you have faith that carries you through the tumult of tantrums thrown by your children? Do you have faith that carries you down the road with a bounce in your step in spite of the fact your car broke down and you've been walking a mile? Do you have faith that responds with joy even though the bill collector's are calling and you have nothing to send to them but your prayers because you've lost your job? Do you have faith even though your friends have left you behind?

Do you have this kind of faith? Do you have Paul's kind of faith? Do you have faith in Jesus?

Do you see the vision of God's Love on Earth? Do you see lives changing because of God's love? Do you see the vision of hearts opening for the Lord? Do you see the vision of everything that breathes praising the Lord? Do you see the surrender of every heart and will to the Father? Do you see the forgiveness of every sin because every mouth has confessed the name of Jesus? Do you see the Holy City that awaits you?

We do not belong to this world, my friends. Paul calls us "transients." In other words, we're just passin' through. We know that something more awaits for us.

We are looking for our true home. And while we look, we're trying to show others the way home as well. We must stand up tall and share our faith. We must boldly proclaim the name of Jesus though the waves are high and land is far away. We must praise even more loudly during these times so that those around us can see the Great Big Awesome God we serve. We must do so, so that others can come to have this same unwavering faith in Jesus.

A faith that tells us that we're just passin' through...a faith that tells us there's something more...a faith that tells us that God goes with us no matter what...a faith that changes lives...a faith in the fact that stuff is going to happen...a faith that leads hearts to Love and be Loved.

Yes, we are transients on this celestial orb...we're just passin' through...but, we are to make the most of our time here by having a faith that believes in what is not yet in hand.

Yes, we are just passing through...but we are not yet through passing.

THE LEAP TO GREATNESS

Luke 22:24-26

grew up for most of my childhood in the 70s and 80s. During the time I grew up, BMX bikes were just being introduced to the world. And as soon as they were introduced, we began to push them to their limit. We would jump over just about anything on our bikes...including each other!

We would brag to each other about who could jump the best, the highest, the longest, over the most people...and on and on. We Loved to brag about our daring flights of fancy.

I remember one occasion when we set up a jump and we were seeing who could jump the farthest. In fact, we set up the jump at the edge of the ditch in the front of our house to give us some extra height. We would go about half way down our street and then pedal like crazy. We would hit that jump and be launched into flight. And when we set that jump up at the edge of the ditch, we would be around six feet in the air and would fly for fifteen to twenty feet sometimes.

At this time in my life, I had outgrown my BMX bike and so I customized my ten-speed to make it a jumping bike. I raised the seat, and flipped the handlebars up so I could stand and pedal harder and faster and use the handlebars to stabilize myself in flight. It was certainly not designed for how I used it ... but I could definitely fly further than anyone else because of the speed I could attain by using the gears of the ten-speed. You could just about see the strain I put on the welded joints of my bike frame each time I landed from a jump. My jumps were never the prettiest. But I didn't care about that. I cared that I could beat everyone else and go higher and farther than anyone on our block.

And because I could do this, everyone on my block did everything in his or her power to beat me. I had set a standard...a dangerous one. All that mattered to me was that I was the best. All that mattered to everyone else was beating my record. And they went to great lengths to do so. (Pun intended.)

One kid on our block was about to do just that. He had been practicing. He had learned how to do a bunny-hop with his BMX bike. A bunny-hop, for those of you who never experienced this part of childhood, is where you're riding along on a flat surface, and you keep your feet planted on your pedals, and then you jump with your body, and it lifts the bike off the ground as well. Bernie was his name. And he learned the bunny-hop. And he figured, that if he timed it just right, he could bunny-hop at the peak of the jump, giving himself extra height, therefore, extra distance.

He was right.

But he couldn't land the jump. The bunny-hop caused him to lose control and he came down on his front tire. For those of you reading who never experienced jumping your bike, landing on your front tire is bad—*very* bad. Bernie ended up flipping over his handlebars and landing on his head. His forward momentum propelled his body over his head and his neck bent backwards at a very un-natural angle.

We stood there aghast at what we were witnessing. We were sure that one of our BMX comrades was about to have a memorial plaque made for him and mounted on the mailbox by the side of the road saying, "Bernie, brave BMXer, died trying to break the record."

The group stood there and suddenly the record didn't matter anymore. All that mattered was Bernie. We flocked to his side to see if he was okay. He was. We exhaled the breath we had collectively been holding since the moment his bike launched off the end of the jump.

The disciples were trying to outdo each other as well. And they stood there that day, bickering over which one of them would be the greatest. They stood there arguing over who's the best, when Jesus had just told them that one of them would be the worst. They had missed the point. They were arguing over something that could never be. Each of them wanted to be the greatest. And that place of honor is reserved at God's right hand for one person only: God's Son. So the disciples argued about that place of honor...and then Jesus reminded them of their place.

"Hey doofuses, you're all wanting to be the best, right? Well, the only way to be the best is to serve the worst. I came to you guys to serve you all. You all think I'm the greatest, and you're right, but look at the example I set for you! I don't strut around acting like the greatest. Instead, I serve the lowest so they can be raised up. You can only be great when you act like you're not and you serve those who are not. Get a clue!"

My friends, take a look around you. Who do you see? Do you see anyone that you're trying to out-do? Who are the people in your life that you're trying to out-do? List them right now.

And now ask yourself "How can I serve them? What can I do for them that might open their eyes to seeing the Kingdom of God?"

As soon as you're able to forget about your own greatness and help others to achieve it, you will have achieved greatness yourself.

The leap to true greatness comes in falling to your knees. It comes from a servant-heart. It comes through humility.

P.S. From that day forward, Bernie's neck could bend in ways that were un-natural to most people. He probably would've been a good gymnast. Maybe even the greatest? But he never bragged about it.

I Love You, Daddy

Hebrews 9:24-28

"My eldest son is a collector. He collects stuff. Coins, cards, books, shells, information. You name it, he collects it. Takes after his old man a bit in this regard.

Occasionally, when I've not been around a lot, or when he's gone through a period of disobedience, he tries to buy my Love. I've got to tell you, that each time this occurs, I experience great emotion. Man, it breaks my heart sometimes to see my young boy standing in front of me, offering me one of his most prized possessions. You see, in these moments, when he's vying for my attention and Love, he almost always takes one of his most valued items in one of his collections to offer to me. There have been times when I've knelt down in front of him to receive the gift that comes from his Love. In some moments, I know it would hurt him more to have me refuse the gift than to receive it. But most of the time, I get down to his level, look in his little brown eyes, and tell him how proud I am of him, how much I Love him, and that he doesn't need to give me anything. I Love him a ton already.

And the most precious words a dad can ever hear often come at these moments: "I Love you, Daddy."

Tears come to me as I write this. Because I know the heart that beats within my son. I know of his Love for me.

And to see him take something so precious unto himself and present it unto me knocks my heart for a loop.

My son is willing to sacrifice what is most precious to him to show his Love for me.

And God was willing to sacrifice what was most precious to him, for us: his only son. God is willing to sacrifice what is most precious to him, to show his Love for us.

What a great reversal! For all of time, God required sacrifices from his children to show their devotion. But then the practice became a set of hoops through which to jump. People began to follow the sacrificial codes to the letter of the law and left a major part of the sacrifice out: their hearts. They began to select their animal sacrifices based upon what satisfied the requirements, rather than out of their devotion to God. For you see, Love is not about checking the box.

And you know, God is so gosh-darned cool that he dove into history to lend a helping hand in the matter. A sacrifice was still required to fulfill the covenant. But it didn't say who could or could not provide it!

So God did. He provided the ultimate, rock 'em, sock 'em, one-two punch, once-and-for-all sacrifice in the form of his one and only Son. The sacrifice of his son fulfilled the sacrificial covenant once and for all, opening the door for all of God's children all around the world to be in a Love-relationship with him.

And yet we still find ourselves doing the same things those legalistic folks of old did. We try to find the lowest common denominator that will fulfill our discipleship responsibilities for the week. We go to church sometimes, not because we're madly in Love with God, but to fulfill our spiritual duty. We serve in ministry not out of the compassion of the Heart of the Father, rather to appease the guilt we carry of the commercialistic lifestyles we lead. Sometimes, I wonder if God looks down with tears flowing down his face contemplating the possibility that the sacrifice of his son was in vain. Because we still don't get it.

Yet, there are those whose hearts that have truly been transformed through the Love and power of the sacrifice that God made on our behalf. And they try to offer a sacrifice anyway. I know I've done this. I've promised God things that I possess to show him my devotion. I promise to dedicate my money, my time, even my possessions as a sacrifice.

And then God kneels down in front of us, with tears streaming down his face to say to our child-like hearts: "I am so proud of you. You are so very precious to me and I Love you from the depths of my God-hood. You don't need to give me anything to show your Love for me or to receive my Love. I Love you a ton already!"

And in that moment, we truly realize there really is nothing we *can* give...nothing we can sacrifice...because God has already made the sacrifice on our behalf. We realize as God looks in our eyes, that the only thing he really wants from us is our Love. The only sacrifice that comes close to being worthy is to give God our hearts.

And so we respond with the most precious words a Dad can ever hear: "I Love you, Daddy."

IF YOU'RE HAPPY AND YOU KNOW IT...

2 Corinthians 8:1-3

hen we were kids, we used to sing a song called, *If You're Happy and You Know It*. It was fun, because we got to sing, clap, stomp, and shout. We were kids, and here, in this song, the grown-ups said: "Go for it! Make a racket. You don't have to be quiet for this one. Give it your best shot. Clap. Stomp. And shout!"

Well, that was good enough for me. I got into this one. I Loved it. And even in times when I wasn't all that happy and I knew it, when we got to sing this song, something changed for me. I became happy.

Happiness is illusive. It's even hard to define. But I think happiness is a childlike joy. Happiness is all of the cutesy things you can think of: puppy dogs, yellow smiley faces, and gold-foil stars. Happiness is a Bomb-pop from the ice cream man in July. Happiness is stomping in mud puddles. Happiness is a hug. Happiness is hard to pin-down, but you know it when you feel it.

And so the song invites you to clap your hands if you know you're happy. And even if you're not, a few claps and stomps later and you find happiness welling up within you.

Jesus tells us to have faith like a child. And happiness is a part of that faith, I truly believe. And somewhere along the way, we are convinced that happiness, instead of being child-*like*, is child-*ish*. And being child-ish, of course, is unacceptable. We must "grow up." We convince ourselves we must leave behind child-ish ways and face the world without the benefit of happiness. And if we don't convince ourselves, Satan whispers it and finally shouts it loudly enough through our alarm clocks, time-cards, pay-checks, overtime, overcharges, overkill, and over-filled calendars that in the end, we must succumb.

Or so we are led to believe...

Paul, in his second correspondence to the church he helped start in Corinth, tells of some other churches in Macedonia who are going through terrible times. If any church should not be happy, it's these churches in Macedonia. They faced terrible hardship and persecution. And yet, Paul says, they "show their true colors." They're happy.

How can this be?

I believe they are happy because they have not left behind or maybe have re-discovered child-like faith and wonder. When asked the question: "What color is the sky in the world you live in?" They always respond with a smile on their face, "Why, rainbow-colored, of course!" And the rest of us cynical old-farts scowl and grumble to each other declaring them naive, pronouncing our sourpuss judgments upon them.

And the more we scowl, the more *they* smile!

Do you remember the time in your life when if you flapped hard enough, you really could fly? When a shot from a loaded finger really could kill people? When an old pop bottle and a stick was the source of a symphony and prophetic visions flowed from crayons? When wondrous healing occurred with a simple kiss? When your covers could repel the foulest of monsters?

You see, child-like faith understands happiness and in fact, fully endorses it. You see, there I go, "endorse." What a grown-up concept. Okay, let's forget endorsements...

Kids know happiness and live it.

And somewhere along the way, it was stripped from us...stolen from our hearts...raped from our souls. And Satan smiled a lascivious smile as he ravished our innocence.

The Macedonian churches were able to respond to their hardship with happiness because they never left it behind. And they knew its source: their Best Friend with whom they pinky-swore that they'd Love each other always...Jesus.

G.K. Chesterton says this: "It may be that God has the eternal appetite for infancy. For we have sinned and grown old, and our Father is younger than we."

We grew up and left happiness behind. We thought it silly, absurd, beneath us, even. And we sinned in that. Because in leaving happiness behind, we leave the heart of the Father behind. We clap away the image of our Father in us as we responsibly clap our hands to turn off the lights. We stomp on the image of our Father in us like a smoldering fire that has become a nuisance. We shout at the image of our Father in us like we're shouting at someone who has cut us off in traffic.

And when we leave such happiness behind, in the tough situations like the Macedonian churches were facing, we can only respond with cynicism, bitterness, and despair.

Close your eyes and go back to the pile of leaves. Look up into the sunshine and feel its joy dancing on your cheeks asking your freckles to come out and play. Remember your best friend. Remember the last "pinky-swear" you made. Imagine popsicle juice running down your chin...no, don't scowl at that...that's a grown-up response...wipe your chin with your sleeve. It's just a shirt...and shirts get washed, right?

If you lived your life like a child, you'd understand that popsicle juice just doesn't matter in the grand scheme of our existence.

LIKE A CHILD

Laughter behind my eyes.
Climbin' trees up to the skies.
Some ask the reasons why,
I say "Because I can."

I'm rubber, you are glue.
Bounce off me, stick to you.
Seven-up, I guess you.
Childhood ways make the man.

And here I stand,
Stand to face the day,
Whatever comes my way.
Like a child,
My life I live,
New Life to you I give.

So so, suck your toe,
All the way to Mexico.
Liar liar, yes I know
The pain you try to hide.

Owen Meany, miny moe.
Always knew which way to go,
Knew which way the wind would blow,
Even on the inside.

And here I stand,
Stand to face the day,
Whatever comes my way.
Like a child,
My life I live,
New Life to you I give.

Olly olly oxen free
Go away and I'll find me.
I will look and I will see
The little boy inside.

Children come to Jesus' knee.
Disciples act like Pharisees.
"Keep away!" "No, come to me!
Have faith like a child."

And here I stand,
Stand to face the day,
Whatever comes my way.
Like a child,
My life I live,
New Life to you I give.

© 1998 by Shane Allen Burton

If you're happy and you know it, clap your hands. Go ahead, I dare ya. Nah...I double-dog dare ya!!! Go for it! Make a racket. You don't have to be quiet for this one. Give it your best shot. Clap. Stomp. And shout Amen! And go have a popsicle while you're at it!

BREAKING THE RULES

Galatians 5:4-6

For much of my life, I have been an ardent rule-follower. If the sign said fifty miles per hour, I would go fifty (notice the past tense). If I was allowed to keep my books from the library for one week, I kept them no longer than one week. Oh yes, for those that know me, this may be hard to believe. But it's true.

It all began when I was a little kid. My parents used to tell me things like, "If you go in the street, you'll get hit by a car and die." And so, I would never play in the street. I believed them. I knew, that if even my shirtsleeve crossed over the boundary of our grass into the cement area of the curb, from out of nowhere, a Mack truck would come screaming by at the speed of sound and take my arm right off, and with blood pluming forth from my stump, I would stumble around in our front yard and die. My parents would then have to put a white cross there with a yellow ribbon on it as a memorial to their beloved child and as a reminder to all children everywhere: "Don't play in the street or you'll get hit by a car and die."

I followed the rules in high school as well. My parents told me horror stories of kids who drank, used drugs and got a hold of some "bad stuff" and died. I believed 'em. I never did drugs, because I knew that I would be the one who would get a hold of something which had a rare, undetectable poison mixed in, and I would consume it and die right there with all the world to see. And people would gather around, as I lay there dead with drug paraphernalia on my person and nod knowingly, "We told him so. He should've known better. He got what he deserved." And they would shake their heads and make "tsk" sounds, clicking their tongues.

And this fear of consequences stuck with me for a while. I bought the whole deal. I was a rule follower and incessantly reminded my parents of the rules: "Mo-om (using two syllables and a whiny voice), you're speeding." Or, "Da-ad, the sign says 'No Smoking.'"

When I was a kid, we lived close enough for me to walk to school. On my very first day, my mom walked me down the driveway to say "goodbye" to me, as I was to head off to school.

We came to the street and I stopped dead in my tracks. My mother's voice echoed in my head: "If you go in the street, you'll get hit by a car and die." I looked up at the woman I knew as my mother and did a little Socratic reasoning: if I go in the street, I'll get hit by a car. If a car hits me, I'll die. My mom is telling me to go into the street where I will surely die. Therefore, my mom is trying to kill me.

My first lesson in the conditionality of rules.

Paul's letter to the church at Galatia was a reminder to remember the conditionality of rules. It was a reminder to remember the heart and intent behind the rules. It was a reminder to remember God's Love.

In my life, rule following hasn't made me a better person. It doesn't matter how many rules I've kept. I could keep every rule and still be a pretty rotten person. What matters is the heart. And the guiding force of the heart is Love. And Love is from God.

Some folks who followed the Jewish law were over-running the churches in Galatia. And they were insisting on returning to the keeping of the codes of the law. In fact, they were judging people at how "good" they were in their faith by how well they kept the law...at how well they followed the rules.

Paul's reminder here is a good one: "Hey folks, it doesn't matter how well you follow the rules. All the rule-followin' in the world ain't gonna make God Love you anymore. There is no standard you can possibly attain on your own. One greater than you has already attained the standard. And he set the standard for you. He set the standard and met the standard so you wouldn't have to. If you keep the rules, great. If you don't keep to these old rules, fine. Loving Jesus is what matters above any rule. So, if you're keeping our old rules, make sure you're doing so out of your Love for Jesus. If you're not keeping to these rules, make sure that you're not just thumbing your nose at the old ways...make sure you're living in Love. Don't let these old "religious" busybodies get in your business and confuse the issue. The issue is Love: God's Love for you, and your Love for him. Got it? Good!"

I'm a first-born in the birth order of our family. We first-borns tend towards perfectionism and over-achievement. We always try to not just meet standards, but also beat them. And this letter from Paul to the churches in Galatia is a healthy reminder to us: focus on Jesus...not earthly standards. But don't just focus on Jesus and how he lived life and what he taught. If we were to do just that, we perfectionists would try to mimic his every action and live his life down to the last letter. We're supposed to focus on the Love-relationship Jesus wants to have with us.

If we live with a guiding force of Love in our lives, we will strive towards the heart of God naturally, because it will flow from being in a living, Loving relationship. However, if we simply focus on standards, without a

Love-relationship, we will always find ourselves wanting more and striving to do better.

When we try to meet standards by our own power and might without living in Love, we are cut off from Love. In effect, we are in exile because we trust only in ourselves.

It's only when we trust in Love, surrendering entirely to Love, that we find the standards met, and the Loving embrace of a God who Loves us more than any rule. He met the standards because we couldn't do it on our own.

Ask yourself today: "what am I trying to do to please God and why?" Are you trying to be the best Christian you can be by "volunteering" all of your time to your church? Are you giving more than a tithe to gain God's favor? Are you striving to be the best husband or wife or friend that you can be only for recognition? If we do any of these things for these reasons, we miss the point.

When we Love someone, we do these sorts of things naturally. When we live in Love, we'll serve as a natural outpouring of our Love. No longer do we "volunteer," we serve out of our Love. When we live in Love, we'll give our money to those in need as a natural outpouring of our Love. No longer are we "giving" money to a church, or charity, we're sharing of our abundance because of Love. When we live in Love, we will be the best husband, wife, or friend we can be as a natural outpouring of our Love. No longer do we try to gain anyone's attention because we know we already have it.

God Loves you to pieces whether or not you follow or break any or all of the rules.

Someone once said: "There is nothing you can do to make God Love you any more. And there's nothing you can do to make him Love you any less."

God Loves you to pieces no matter what.

PERFECT 100

Luke 15:1-7

 *J*ust last week, I met a young woman who was a Pharisee. No, she wasn't aware of it. But she was one. In fact, so am I sometimes. And I'll bet you are as well.

I met Allison at an all-night restaurant. We were with some friends on vacation for an extended weekend. We stopped at this restaurant late at night, hungry, and in need of some coffee. We were seated and our server came to offer us drinks.

I have this habit of talking to people—especially people who normally aren't noticed. People like Allison. Ask yourself when the last time was when you got to know your server at a restaurant. When was the last time you knew the server's name by the time you were done with your meal? When was the last time you asked *them* if "everything was okay?" Well, this is my annoying habit. If you've dined with me, you've probably been annoyed by it. But occasionally, something happens. Like what happened that night with Allison.

As soon as she came back with our drinks, the conversation—no, the banter—began. She was a young college student and was kind of sassy. She was a fun person working a job just to pay some bills. She was obviously not having any fun that night. Until we got there. And the conversation flowed so easily, that at one point, she even began to make some jokes at my expense. Her night was being transformed. It went from moping around the restaurant to a casual, spirited banter with some good laughs.

At one point, much later in the conversation, she came back to the table to see how we were doing. At this point, I was asking her if she knew some of the professors I knew at the local college. She asked me how I knew them, and I told her it was because I was a pastor in this town for a few years. I then made some joke about her spending her weekends at one of the local bars that I knew of. To which she responded, "How does a pastor know about this bar?"

And I asked her, "Just what kind of people do you think Jesus spent his time with?"

She said something like, "His disciples."

I said, "Yes, and who else?"

"Religious people?" she said, pretty unsure of herself.

"Nope," I said. And at this point in the conversation, she literally pulled up a chair and sat down with us. She sat there waiting for me to proceed.

"Jesus spent time with bar-people."

"Huh?!" she said surprised.

"Yup. That bar you've gone to? That's exactly the kind of place Jesus would've wanted to go. He didn't like hangin' around 'religious' folks. He wanted to find the people who needed something more. Jesus hung around with prostitutes and tax collectors. He hung around people no one wanted to hang around with. People just like at that bar."

Allison smiled at that point. The Message had been conveyed. But I pray that it lived on in Allison's heart.

Love.

Extravagant Love from a God who loves the least, the last, and the lost, so they will become the most, the first, and the found.

Jesus was confronted by the Pharisees for hangin' out with the "bar-people." And in classic Jesus-style, he told them a story. He told them of a shepherd who would leave ninety-nine sheep to go find the one that was lost. The Pharisees were supposed to get the point. They were supposed to realize *they* were the ninety-nine and the bar-people were the one lost sheep. And if they had half a brain between them, I suspect they *did* get the point and probably didn't like it. They were probably offended even more.

But I hope not. I've got this crazy notion that maybe some of the Pharisees weren't as cold as we make them out to be. I've got this notion that some of the Pharisees were actually more like the one sheep than the ninety-nine. Yeah, when you put the Pharisees together as a group, they looked down their noses at humanity. Just as we so often do when we're together in our groups of ninety-nine.

"Who me?" you ask.

Yup. And you know what? Me too. Yeah, I so very often look down my nose at humanity. I so easily get caught up in a person's faults and I end up forgetting whose child they are. God's. Not mine. I'm a brother to them...not the Father.

And it's much easier to put others down, than it is to build them up. It's much easier to get together with our groups of friends and stand around berating others for not being like us. It's so much easier to do so, in a vain attempt to make ourselves feel better than it is to invite them into our groups in a valiant attempt at making *them* feel better.

My friends, you and I, we're the "found" sheep. We're often the very Pharisees Jesus was talkin' about. And lest we forget this, we should take time to remember the last person at whom we looked down our noses. How long ago was it? Maybe it was just before you opened this book and found this very devotional as you looked across your place of work and saw *that* person? Maybe it was on your way to work and you saw someone picking his or her nose in the car next to you? Maybe it was that homeless person you saw when you were downtown? Maybe it was a relative you saw having too much to drink? Maybe it was your boss, your wife, your husband, your friend, your child, or your pastor?

Think of that person right now. If you are part of the ninety-nine that Jesus is talkin' about, they are the one. Go find them. Get it right between you. And if they don't know Jesus, begin working towards that reality. Infuse your relationship with prayer. Start praying that God would open the door to you being able to share Jesus with them.

Us ninety-nine, we gotta stick together. Because we've been found. And we must not forget that at one point, we were the one. We aren't any better. And the ninety-nine, they stood there all together looking down their noses at us. We have been the object of the ninety-nine's scorn. We have been the subjects of their ridicule. We have been excluded from all their reindeer games. So now that we're a part of the ninety-nine, let's not get all high & mighty on the one.

Because without the one, we can never be a perfect 100.

It says in the Scripture that the Shepherd said, "Woo hoo!" when he found the lost sheep and called his friends and neighbors together to celebrate. He's celebrating the completion of his flock of sheep. When the ninety-nine realize their relationship to the one and repent...and when the one realizes his or her relationship to The One and repents, the flock is made perfect.

A perfect 100.

'Munion, Daddy?

John 13:21-27

ears ago, I played drums on a worship team in Fargo, Nort Dakota (I left the "h" out on purpose). Our worship leader was a man of God named Eric. He was a great husband, father, worship pastor, and friend. And though it has been eleven years since I have had the privilege of worshiping with him, I am blessed still by having known him. I learned a lot from his worship leading and friendship. And of the greatest things I learned had to do with Communion: eating the bread, drinking the juice or wine, sharing in God's tremendous gift of Love through his Grace.

Eric came to one worship rehearsal and told us a story about something that had happened when his son was about two or three years old. One night, Eric was giving his son a bath. He ran the water, got the soap ready, and put his little boy in the tub, at which point, he knelt down at the side of the tub. His son with a somewhat perplexed look on his face looked up into his daddy's eyes and said, "'Munion, daddy?"

Eric was also confused by this. Everyone who's had a two-year-old or three-year-old knows that once in a while, you have a hard time understanding what the toddler is saying.

And so gently, Eric said, "What?"

And his son, with deep meaning, looked again into his daddy's eyes and said, "'Munion, daddy."

As the look of realization slowly crept upon his face, so did a tear appear in his eyes as Eric connected the dots. His son saw his father kneeling and assumed that it was time for Communion. Something profound had occurred. And Eric, led by the Holy Spirit, went to the kitchen, got some juice and a slice of Wonder Bread and knelt again at the side of the bathtub with 'Munion.

"This is the body of Jesus, broken for you and his blood shed for you because Jesus Loves you, son."

A holy moment indeed. I have to believe that God pays special attention when his children begin to understand the depth of his Love for them.

I am so grateful for the lesson I learned from Eric in this story. Because Eric didn't have to react the way he did. He could've simply smiled a cute smile at his son and proceeded with a normal bath time. Instead, he followed the prompting of the Holy Spirit and opened up the Holy Table of his Heavenly Father to a boy who was open to receiving the gift of 'Munion.

In fact, because of his example, I started giving Communion to my children as soon as they had cut their teeth. Because children can understand that it's a special meal. They can understand the words "Jesus Loves you." And truly, even if you ask the greatest pastors and theologians to explain what happens in Communion, they will try with large words to explain what occurs. And yet one wise theologian was asked to sum up all of his theology and did so in his thick German accent by saying simply, "Jesus Loves me, ziss I know, for zee Bible tells me so."

It's not that complicated, really. We can use big words. Or we can use Jesus' words: "This is my body broken for you; do this in remembrance of me. This cup is the new covenant in my blood, which is poured out for you. As the Father has Loved me, so I have Loved you."

A special meal where we discover and re-discover that Jesus Loves us. Even a child can understand.

Through the years, I have been to churches where it didn't matter whether or not you were open to receiving the gift of Communion. One church I went to required that you be a member to receive the gift of God's Grace in Communion. Another church required registration. Yes, you had to fill out a registration card to take Communion and if you were not on the list, you didn't get to share in God's Love. Some churches say that if you're divorced you are not eligible to receive the bread and the juice. Others say that you have to wait until you are a certain age, until you're baptized, until you're confirmed...until you put your right foot in and your right foot out and then shake it all about.

The Hokey Pokey comes from the words *hocus pocus,* which come from the Latin, *hoc est corpum*...the body of Christ. A long time ago, people couldn't understand all the actions and words priests were doing when celebrating Communion and misunderstood the words to be hocus pocus that was then satirized in a children's game, called the Hokey Pokey.

You don't have to put your right foot in, be a certain age, or be a member. You come because you have a need. You need Grace. You need to depend on something larger than yourself...some One larger than yourself. You need a hand. You need to belong to a family. You need forgiveness. You need Love. You need a Savior. You come to the table in a worthy manner when you come with a need. You come in a worthy manner when you recognize you belong to the Body of Christ. You come in a worthy manner when you come with reverence, awe, and worship. Sometimes you come to the Table knowing your sins. And sometimes, coming to the Table convicts you of your sins. But every time you come, you are *forgiven* for your sins.

Take a closer look at the Scripture. Read the whole chapter if you have the time. In it, you will find Jesus passing the bread and the wine around so that everyone would have some. Every one. And Jesus says in advance that the one who will dip his bread with Jesus will be the one who betrays him. Jesus knows in advance, that we're going to sin and still he offers us the gift of his Love and Grace.

Even Judas got the bread.

Jesus offered Judas Communion. And lest we forget, there was at least one other betrayer in the room that night. It was on him that the foundation of the Church as we know it today was built. His name? Peter. Haven't we all been Judas and Peter at one point or another? Haven't we all denied and betrayed our Lord? If you deny this, then you deny your sin. For every time we sin, we crucify Christ.

We cast our taunts along with our stones...we bow in mock worship...*we* pound the nails.

Who are we to deny Communion to someone who comes in a time of need...for aren't we all in need as well?

Look closely...it is us there next to Jesus dipping bread with him. And it should be us there in that bathtub as well with our Heavenly Father kneeling down beside us. We need to be washed clean. And as we look up to our Daddy with wondering eyes...somewhat perplexed at the depth of his Love, we come to a place where words escape us. We come to a place where all of the big words in the longest books will do us no good.

We come to a place of need where we can only ask, "'Munion, Daddy?"

JELLIED CRANBERRY BLESSINGS

1 Peter 4:7-11

My favorite food on the planet is jellied cranberries. You know, that cylindrically shaped maroon hunk of tart-tasting jellied substance that glops out of the can into a bowl upon which time, you cut it into half-inch slices to await your dining pleasure. Yes, strangely enough, this is my favorite food. It has been all the way back to kindergarten when Mrs. Bonde invited us all to draw our favorite food. I colored a red circle. She thought that I didn't get the assignment and so she failed my drawing. (*Can you do that in kindergarten?!*)

When we had parent-teacher conferences, Mrs. Bonde expressed her concern over my development because I didn't understand how to draw my favorite food. My parents started laughing as soon as they saw the picture. They knew what it was and they understood why she didn't get it. I remember days in school when we had jellied cranberries. Most kids couldn't stand 'em. Those days were happy days for me!

"Pass your cranberries down to Shane! He'll take 'em all!"

I remember another time when they had served beets at school for lunch. They, too, were maroon slices. I took one bite and well, that was the end of lunch for me and several others sitting around me.

There are times when I will purchase a small can of this delectable slime, pop it open, and down it in a couple of bites. (If you're feeling ill right now, please take a break...it gets better...or worse, depending upon your point of view on jellied cranberries!) I Love this stuff. And now we're coming to the one week out of the year when I have permission to down as much of this stuff as I can possibly handle. My favorite thing to do is to get some wonderful turkey gravy and pour it over the cranberries. MMMmmm...that mixture of salty gravy and sweet, tart cranberries...I'm salivating.

But you know what? I take my cranberries for granted. I just assume each Thanksgiving that they'll be there. I take turkey, stuffing, mashed potatoes, gravy, corn, and especially jellied cranberries for granted. Sometimes I take my four children for granted. I just assume they'll be there no matter what. I often take my car and my house for granted as well. I just assume that when I put the key in the ignition that some fuel will be injected into the cylinder, which will compress it and a spark will then ignite it creating a small explosion and the internal combustion process will begin and I will be on my way. I assume that when I come home, I will enter a warm house with cupboards that have food in them. I take my friends for granted, just assuming that they'll be there, even if I'm not. In fact, I even take God for granted sometimes...leaving him the leftovers of my life asking him to tidy things up for me.

In this first letter from Peter, he reminds us that we're living in a time when everything is about to be wrapped up...we don't know the hour or the day...but it's going to happen sometime. He's reminding us that because of this, we are to take nothing for granted...*nothing*. Don't even take your e-mail for granted. Don't take the chair you're sitting upon for granted. Don't take friends or family for granted. Don't take simple pleasures for granted. Don't take jellied cranberries for granted...and certainly don't take God for granted.

He says that we're supposed to Love each other as if our lives depended on it. And my friends, I believe that they do. I believe our lives do depend on us Loving each other. Because there will come a time in all of our lives, that something or someone we take for granted will not be there at the critical moment, and in that moment, our lives may very well depend upon the Love we have for each other.

And certainly, there are those around us whose lives will depend on whether or not we Love in this way. Certainly, this cold week before Thanksgiving, there are many who took much for granted, only to find themselves sorely lacking, not feeling very much like they have much for which to be thankful.

As we gather with family and friends to stuff ourselves like the very turkeys we'll consume, there will be many who would feel stuffed if they even had one of the dinner rolls we'll toss away when we're all done because they haven't had the luxury of a full meal in days. We're going to have leftovers for days from the one meal we'll consume this Thursday. While many will have only the leftovers from a dumpster upon which to dine as their very meal for which they'll give thanks. I'm not exaggerating.

Peter's reminder here to us is that God has given us a bounty of blessings of which we are not to hoard unto ourselves, but to share generously with those around us. If we share of that with we which are blessed, it will be as if the very hands of God had reached out to those in need to give them food for their bellies, a blanket for their cold bodies, a place to stay other than the cold streets upon which we ride in our chariots of gold. When we share a kind word, it is as if the mouth of God has spoken a blessing. When the Love of Jesus Christ is allowed to well up within us, it will pour forth from our hearts and spill out into all those around us.

When we stop and take stock of all with which we have been blessed, including the endless Love of the Father as expressed through the life, death, and resurrection of his Son Jesus, we cannot help but for our hearts to break for humanity in the same way God's heart breaks.

What do you take for granted? Make a list today of that which you take for granted. And then make time and take time to thank God for those things in your life. And when you look at your list and you see the people you take for granted, then why don't you thank them for being who they are to you?

Peter tells us not only to stop taking things for granted, but also to share these very things with those in need. It is not enough to simply feel badly for those whose plights are worse than ours. We are to take action. We are to be generous with our words, yes. But we are to be generous with all with which we have been blessed. We are to feed the hungry. We are to give a bed to the homeless...and we are to do so cheerfully.

This Thanksgiving, as you dine with those you Love, remember what it is to be thankful. Remember your blessings. Praise God for them. Do not let yourselves take anyone or anything for granted. Tell the people you Love that you Love them. Praise God for the food. Praise God for your life. And ask God to open the eyes of your heart to see the world around you in the way that he sees it so you will be able to see the opportunities you are being given each day to be generous with all that God has given you.

I'll bet you never thought that jellied cranberries could be so profound, huh? But when they're passed around the table this year, stop and praise God for 'em, even if you don't like 'em. Let them be a reminder to you...let them be a symbol of blessing. When the cranberries come to you, stop for a moment and praise God.

Pass the cranberries! Oh, yeah, could I get some gravy, too?

BEAR MUCH FRUIT

Romans 11:16-24

*A*nd there you were, a lone little olive shoot, strug-
gling to gather moisture in the arid heat of the
desert. The ground around you is dry and cracked,
parched beyond what should be possible. You stretch your
arms to the sky in prayer. Every day, your eyes search the
Heavens for any signs that your prayers for rain have
been heard. You plead with the Heavens, and most days,
the only answer you hear is the howling of the wind. You
are trying so very hard to bear fruit, but without the
sustenance you need, you are unable. If someone were to
pass by, what evidence would there be that you were an
olive tree? Without fruit, how would they tell?

And your roots, they are so weak in this dry wasteland. They are not connected under the ground with the
roots of other olive shoots. And so when the wind tears
across the barren ground, it tears at your very being,
threatening to pull you unwillingly from the ground in
which you grow. You are afraid that one day, you will not
be able to hold on any longer. You will have to let go and
let yourself be buffeted about on the screaming wind that
tears at the edge of your consciousness.

Each day, the scorching sun sears the horizon of your
consciousness, and each day you persist in throwing your
arms towards Heaven in your plea for water. Just a little.
One drop would be wonderful. As you stretch your arms

up, you often wonder why you're here. How did you even get here? Were you put here for a reason? Or did some traveler just happen to be eating an olive and it's seed serendipitously fell upon this patch of earth? For some reason or no reason, you are here. And you are growing. And you are still alive. And so you still hope.

One day a raven flits down next to you. From a height, it saw you there and thought that it might rest its wings in your branches. But upon flying nearer, it realized your size and knew its weight could not be supported by your measly existence. Feeling a new note of hope singing upon your heartstrings, you boldly say "hello."

Instead of a greeting, you only hear the heartless cackle of the cruel laughing world from which this raven has come. The raven asks, "What are you, anyway?"

You reply with certainty, "An olive shoot."

"Yeah, right." says the raven. "And I'm an eagle."

"No...really. I am an olive shoot. And one day I'll be a tree." You respond, trying to build confidence in the face of this mocking fowl.

Scoffing, the raven laughs at you and jeers, "Sure you will, little branch. You just keep dreaming your dreams, and one day you'll find that you will wake up in the middle of this desert, and you will still be only this pitiful excuse for a shoot. You'll never be a tree. How could you? There's nothing out here! You'll never make it on your own." And the raven looks up to Heaven and laughs.

As he laughs, you realize he's right. There's no way you'll make it on your own out here. It's too dry. You have no one else's roots to hold to give you strength. You will never be a tree. Seeing the look of defeat in you, the raven stretches it's sinister wings and launches itself into flight.

Ah, if only you could fly. Then you could find a fertile piece of land upon which to grow. You could find a source of water. You could find others like you to support you as you grow. Again, hope soars within you. And as it does, the sun begins to set. And you realize in that setting moment, the raven is right. But his rightness is not cause to abandon hope. His rightness is reason to begin praying for something else. You realize that you've been praying for what you *thought* you needed. And the answer you've been receiving over and over is "no." You've been praying for the wrong thing. Yeah, sure, you need water to grow. But there's something you need even more. And so as the sun travels along its way, signaling the end of this good day, you rest in the comfort that there will be a new dawn, upon which you fly.

You awaken to the sounds of an early morning breeze that heralds the coming of a storm. A new excitement wells up within you as you realize that today is the day! As the sun stretches over the horizon, you stretch your arms once again to Heaven in prayer. This time your prayer is different. You're not praying for sustenance. You're not praying for water. You're not praying for anything that will help you to make it on your own. Because herein has been your error: you've been praying for things that will help you to maintain your independence. Silly olive shoot!

Your prayer is new today. It sings forth from within you! "Father of us all," you pray, "I realize that I am a pitiful excuse for an olive shoot. Truly, you have made me and I am a blessing. But I cannot grow by myself. I need you. And so today, I will let go of all that I hold on to. And I will trust myself in your hands, as you carry me upon your Breath. Take me. Use me. Do what you will with me. I surrender myself entirely to You, Father."

As you breathe the last words of your prayer, as your face is upturned to Heaven, you feel the smile of the Father as he breathes life into the world around you. And as the winds increase, your soul begins to sing in harmony with the Breath of God. You feel the energy building. The storm is growing. You must wait just a little longer. It's hard to wait, now that you know what you must do. But it's not quite right just yet. Hold. Wait. Just a little more. The wind has almost reached the intensity it will need to be able to bear you aloft. And as the wind crescendos, your roots release their grip on the arid earth, and the symphonic storm bears you up on the very Breath of God.

You look down and you see the desert of your existence passing you by. You see the old familiar wasteland leaving. For a brief moment, you are tempted to dive back to the familiarity of the desert. But you look up and hear the song of the Father in the wind around you and so you trust yourself to the journey on which you are being taken.

Finally, the winds begin to subside. You hear one word breathed into the storm: "Peace." And as mightily as the storm crescendoed, it now fades into echoes as you are brought gently to rest upon a new ground. As soon as you feel it, you sense its difference. It courses with life! And there is moisture here of which you've never tasted its like. You lay upon this new ground with a new sense of purpose. You rest. A deep soul sigh softly escapes your lips as you soar into dreams of your new life.

As you awaken, you realize now, that you are not alone. There are mighty olive trees standing tall all around you! Oh, to be such a tree! And you notice, that upon each and every branch, there is fruit! All around the base of the trees, you see the dead branches that have been cut away. You see the branches that have not born fruit. You have a desire to be such a tree as these: bearing the fruit to which you have been born to bring forth.

A sudden moment of panic overcomes you as you realize your roots are exposed to the air. No matter how you twist and turn, you can't get them to reach to the ground. You are helpless. The panic grows. "No!" You scream. "How can this be? I let go. I surrendered! What more do you want?" You scream into the stillness of this new day...this good day. And as you lay there, heaving sobs of grief, you hear the sound of footsteps in this garden of glory.

It's the Gardener. And as he goes to each tree, you see the care with which he tends each one. You see the Love in his eyes. You see the tender sureness of his hands as he carefully examines the branches. You see the sadness in his eyes as he comes upon a branch that does not bear fruit. He holds the branch tenderly in his Loving hands. His head bows. Great anguish seeps forth from his heart and sobs wrack his body. But he knows what he must do. And he does it with purpose. He reaches to his belt and pulls forth a blade called justice with mercy written upon its handle and he carves at the base of the fruitless branch. Its cries pierce the glory of this good day and you cannot help but to join the Gardener in his grief.

As you lie there sobbing, you sense a new movement. The Gardener is coming toward you. He gently kneels down next to you and carefully lifts you in his care-full hands. He looks back to the mighty olive tree from which he has just severed the fruitless branch and then he looks down at you. An idea breaks forth upon his face evidenced by the smile now replacing the grimace of pain. He carries you to the mighty olive tree. He says to you gently, "This will hurt a bit. But trust me."

You see the glint of the blade he just used a moment ago glisten in the dawning sun and you realize that he intends to use it upon you. A shudder of fear passes through you as you feel its hardness against the base of your roots. And then a pain like which you've never known—not even from the most scorching desert sun— grabs the entirety of your being as the Gardener saws your roots off. You are raw. Sensitive to the slightest breeze. Pain screams along your base. With a questioning look, you gaze into the Gardener's eyes as if to ask "why." And in his kind gaze, you find your answer. "Trust Me." There is a great Love there. And so you do. You trust.

And the Gardener brings the base of your body to his lips to add his healing kiss to your pain. And then as he withdraws his kiss, he places the base of your little body against the tender spot on the mighty olive tree. At first it hurts. But then you begin to feel a glorious song coursing through the veins of this great tree. You feel it singing to you. You feel it in the depths of who you are, and the haunting moments of your loneliest desert hours form complex harmonies with this new song. You are being grafted onto a tree that bears fruit! And you feel the calling deep within you to do the same. You have found your purpose. Your prayers have been heard. All those hours of stretching your arms to Heaven were not in vain. Because in doing so, you learned from whence your life does truly come.

Now the Gardener is binding you to his tree. And even as he does this, you begin to feel yourself becoming one with it...one with him. You feel living water coming from the tree and into your little body. And you feel the new life to which you are called already growing you beyond what you ever were in the desert. You know your purpose. You know Hope. You know you will grow fruit. And you know the Father's Love. You've felt it...as he severed the roots of your independence and grafted you to a fruit-bearing tree.

Bear fruit, my dear friend! Bear it well, for as people pass by, they will only know that you are an olive tree, by the fruit you bear. They will only know the Gardener by his trees and their fruit.

HEY, CUZ!

Luke 1: 36-42

*H*ere is a small fact that gets glossed over each Advent. God's holy angel, Gabriel, comes to give news to Mary and while talking to her about the Savior she will bear, makes reference to her relative Elizabeth. How closely related were they? Luke doesn't say. But, what is important to mention, is that Mary and Elizabeth are indeed related.

At some level, that makes Jesus, Son of Mary and Joseph—Son of God—the cousin of John, later known as The Baptist.

I got to thinking, what were family reunions like? What was it like for these two cousins? John knew who Jesus was...who he would be come...who he is still today. It says, "He leaped in her womb." When Mary, mother of the Savior, walked into the room, John, as an unborn baby, recognized her. He knew her role. He knew the Child she would bear.

He knew.

So as children growing up, John knew. When Mary and Elizabeth would get together, John knew. I imagine that childhood games weren't all that much fun. "Red rover, red rover, send...God right over." Or can you imagine hide and go seek? Jesus wouldn't even have to go look. I'll bet they never had to play *Eeny-Meany-Miny-Moe* to choose who would be "it." All they had to do was ask Jesus. And do you think Jesus and John ever went to a fishing hole together? There's John, sitting on the shore, waiting for even a nibble, while Jesus strolls right out on the water, reaches down, and grabs a fish. Could they play guessing games?

Did they ever try and count the stars...and succeed? Did John know one day he would get beheaded? If he didn't know, did Jesus tell him? Did Zechariah and Joseph ever have to forego sparing the rod in the aftermath of any Baptist & Savior shenanigans? Did John and Jesus ever wrestle? Did Jesus win fairly, or did he sometimes let John win to be a good sport? Did Elizabeth and Mary ever look at the Baptist and the Savior and say, "Boys will be boys?" Was John ever envious of Jesus? Did they ever fight? Did John ever give God a bloody nose? And then think to himself, "Oops." Were they ever grounded?

What dreams did they dream...what stories did they tell? Did Jesus ever use his divinity to get out of taking a bath? When they stomped in puddles, did John notice the far away look in Jesus' eye as he remembered creating the oceans and seas? Did he ever lord his lordship over his mom and dad, "You just wait until you get home to your Father!"

Years later, when John is in the water, baptizing people and here comes Jesus, it's no wonder John recognizes Jesus. No wonder at all. They're family. John knew Jesus...from the time he was a babe. And so as John's disciples were repenting and getting baptized, he immediately knew the Man walking down the shore towards them.

Do you see the twinkle in Jesus' eyes? Our mischievous Savior walks right up into the midst of this mottled crowd and says, "Hey, cuz" with a knowing nod of His head. Oh, the words aren't there in the Bible...I've looked. But can't you just hear something like that coming from the Savior? Something so familiar...so Loving...so unheard of coming from the Almighty and yet, that's the kind of startling Savior we have. He shows up when we least expect it, but most need it.

Did you catch that last phrase?

Here it is again...read it slowly, and over and over again if you need to. Let it really sink in.

Jesus shows up when we least expect it, but most need it.

He showed up when I was depressed. He showed up when I was broke. He showed up when I got divorced. He showed up when I denied him. He showed up for my greatest celebrations...and my greatest failures.

He even showed up when I didn't.

Jesus shows up when we least expect it, but most need it.

That's what Advent is all about...God showing up when we least expect him, but most need him. God diving into human history to swim through the mire of our ways and rescue us in spite of ourselves.

I have a question for you today, my friend: Are you expecting him? Because you know what? He's going to show up...whether you think you need him or not. Another question, why do you need him right now? Are you down and out? Are you unemployed? Have you abandoned your family, or they you? Are you underpaid and overdrawn? Are your credit cards already maxed out with false perceptions of "need?" Do you crave a drink or a toke more than you do your next breath...more than you do your Savior? Have empty wanton promises of lust left you wanting and waiting for something more?

What are you waiting for isn't the right question. No, the question is: "Who are you waiting for?" Who? Friend, there's only one name I can think of that will do. Don't look now; is that him walking towards you? He strolls right up to you, nods his head, and with a twinkle in his eyes, he says, "Hey, cuz!"

It's true, isn't it? We're all a part of his family.

God showing up when we least expect it, but most need it to remind us of the family to which we belong.

You nod your head...unsure at first...hoping, no, praying Jesus is the answer to all of your questions...the healing to your greatest wounds...you look at him. Everyone has stopped and observes. What will happen next? It's up to you. Do you recognize yourself as part of God's family, or do you keep on walking, ignoring this Man...this God who has disrupted your self-pity, your searching, and your solicitation.

You have tried all your own answers...and failed.

Jesus shows up when we least expect it, but most need it.

Hesitantly, a smile comes to your face. You find the boldness from somewhere to meet his fierce, tender gaze. You see the Man...and recognize the Savior. *Your* Savior.

As you stroll malls searching for sales...as you wait in long-lasting lines...as you ponder your predicaments and procurements...remember what you really need this Christmas...who you really need.

Jesus shows up when we least expect it, but most need it.

A Nod and a Smile

Luke 23:44

This is not usually the time of year when we think of Jesus being crucified. But the other day, when we went for our annual family-hike-for-three-hours-and-saw-your-own-Christmas-tree excursion, one of my children asked me, "Dad, how come we have Christmas trees?" And again, I realized anew the power of this season. For it is not just a birth that we celebrate. It isn't just the incarnation. It is the crucifixion as well, for Jesus was nailed to a tree.

As you set up your trees this year...contemplate not just the birth, but the crucifixion as well. Imagine that day.

The sun beat down upon Jesus' upturned face. The sweat had long since stopped flowing. It had been a long day already. A sleepless night spent praying. A friend giving the kiss of death. Another friend denying friendship. The trial. The crowd setting free a known criminal instead of the Innocent. After the beatings, there was the mocking crowd jeering at him as he passed, the heavy beam upon his back, when put together with another beam would form a symbol that echoes that day even still. The sweat dripped then—*poured* really—as he stumbled along that stony path.

His skin was slick with it as the man Simon from Cyrene stopped to help him carry the instrument of his death. As Simon tried to help him stand, his hands slipped on his skin from the sweat that was still there. But by the time he finally made it to the top of the hill called Skull, there was no more moisture left within him to perspire.

The sun was bright in his eyes. He could still hear the crowd mocking him. He could hear a group of soldiers off to one side, even now dividing up the rags of his symbolic royalty. Little did they know. A captain in the guard stood by—maybe he even helped hold Jesus down—as an innocent Man was nailed to that forsaken piece of wood that day. A captain who, in the last moments, recognized Jesus for who he was.

I wonder about this Captain. It's quite possible that he was about the same age as Jesus. In fact, maybe they even knew of each other as children? Is it possible, that some childhood moments were spent together? Surely, Jesus would've have played with a young Roman boy. What would have been a forbidden friendship may actually have been the sentiment behind the Captain's recognition. Maybe it is, that one day, while playing, the Roman boy was interrupted by another boy. The boy was a little rough around the edges, perhaps. One look at his hands and the Roman boy knew that this other boy was a hard worker. Already, he had the calluses of someone used to manual labor.

"Hi," said the New Boy.

"Hello," replied the young Roman.

"Mind if I play?" asked the New Boy.

"Ah...you're a Jew, aren't you?" asked the Roman boy.

"Yeah, but I don't care if you don't!" said the Jewish Boy with a gleam in his eye. And they grasped each other's hands for the first time...but not the last.

Thus may a friendship have begun that day. Who knows? Could it be that as the two grew, they would watch the other's progress? They would keep track of how each other was doing. Occasionally, though the public would not understand such a friendship, they would catch each other's eye with a knowing nod and smile.

They grew into young men. The boy Jesus following in his earthly father's footsteps and learning the trade of carpentry. The young Roman following in his father's footsteps and becoming a Roman centurion. They excelled in their respective trades, Jesus, becoming a master carpenter, just like his father...the Roman becoming a Captain in the Roman army.

The Captain became married and one day had a child with his wife. The Captain saw an opportunity to check in on his childhood friend. He went to see a Carpenter about getting a cradle for his child. He went to his Friend's shop and commissioned just such a piece. The rough hands he remembered from that one day as children were now larger and even more calloused, but had grown that much more skillful as well. The cradle was beautiful!

And while they could not really acknowledge each other, again, that knowing nod and smile passed between them as the purchase was made.

The rough hands of a Carpenter had crafted something that would cradle the smooth skin of a child. Much smoother than the cradle that had held him as a baby, to be sure.

Is it ironic to think that a lowly, rough-hewn wooden feeding box—a manger—cradled the King of the Universe Who would one day craft the cradles that would hold the babies who would become the Captains and Kings of this world? The Roman Captain and the Carpenter Jesus shook hands on their deal that day...a reminder of the day they first met.

The sun beats down upon the back of the Roman Captain as he looks down upon the face of an old Friend. Sweat still trails down his back, for he has not walked the same path of the Man before him on the ground. His eyes meet those of the Man lying upon the rough-hewn work of another carpenter. They hold each other's gaze for a moment. Mercy in the eyes of Jesus. Shame in the eyes of the Roman Captain. Something draws his face back up to meet the eyes of Jesus again. And this time the Captain sees it: forgiveness. A sob wracks his body...shaking his soul...and he quickly chokes it back in the midst of the taunts around him. He can't let his soldiers see the tear that is forming in his eye as he looks upon a Friend.

A nod and a smile pass between them once again.

And for the last time, they clasp hands, even as the hammer is raised to the sky to drive the nail down through the flesh of the Man on the cross. The Roman Captain has just held down the hand of a Friend so that it could be nailed to the symbol of eternal hope and forgiveness. He rises, as the Man before him on the cross is being raised and dropped into place in the hole that will hold the rude instrument of death.

And as his very own soldiers around him gamble for the garments of his Friend, he hears his Friend breathe his last, uttering words of forgiven finality: "It is finished."

And whether or not his soldiers heard him that day, some in the crowd did, for it is recorded here in Holy Scripture. This Captain—who may have known Jesus in other ways before this day—acknowledged a Friend proclaiming his innocence. And his Friend heard him.

And the King of the Universe, from his perch in the tree, nodded and smiled his forgiveness.

HE DIDN'T HAVE TO DO IT...BUT HE DID

Isaiah 7:14

He didn't have to do it, you know. The Almighty Lord Creator Of All That Ever Was And Ever Will Be didn't have to bother with the likes of us. And he certainly didn't have to do it in the way he did it. But he did. One day, God was contemplating all that he had brought forth into being and it came to be the time that he had planned for all along.

God sat upon the throne of eternity, looking across time and space to see the first wayward choice made by God's first friend upon his creation called earth. And at the very same moment he stared Adam in the face and saw the shame there, God also saw the look his Son would give him at the moment of his ultimate abandonment and betrayal upon his earthly throne...two rough-hewn pieces of wood, lashed together with rope, not crushed red velvet. God also saw in that very same moment the looks on all of the faces that would come to receive his Son in their hearts. From shame to abandonment to the purest rejoicing! And the sight of rejoicing clinched it.

That did it.

God arose from his throne, gathering up the infinity of his divinity, and he squeezed himself into a womb of a young virgin named Mary. What was it like for an infinite Being existing in every moment and in every quark throughout the universe to be confined to such a space?

What was it like for God, Absolute Purity, to enter into sin-stained creation? What did the taint feel like?

He didn't have to do it, you know. The Creator Of Order And Chaos didn't have to bother with the likes of us. Certainly humanity had turned its collective back upon the Divinity from which it had sprung. Certainly, God could have resigned himself to being the Great Watchmaker who created the watch, set it into motion, sitting back to observe history unfold, never entering into it...never bothering to check its accuracy or movement. But he did. He dove right in to bring about a New Order. Several years later, he would gather some of his friends around a table and tell them about this New Order. He would call it a New Covenant. A New Covenant of Grace and Forgiveness that would set things right all the way back to his first friend Adam. But this New Order was also a New Chaos, because he would come and turn everything upside down...from our perspective, anyway.

God...yes God...was in a womb for nine months. Hearing the muffled sounds of life going on around his mother, a young woman named Mary. God heard her prayers from inside her. Imagine that...she's praying, thinking her prayers are drifting off into the ethereal realms of God, and her prayers are being heard from within her. Sure, she'd heard the prophecy of Emmanuel...God with us. But she didn't really understand how with us he'd be.

He didn't have to do it, you know. The Lord Over All And Everything certainly didn't have to become Emmanuel. The Lord who set the universe in motion sitting above it all, aware of every atom, did not have to come to be with us. But he did.

And here's the question...why?

Why did the The Lord Over All And Everything, The Creator Of Order And Chaos, Absolute Purity, The Almighty Lord Creator Of All That Ever Was And Ever Will Be come to be with us?

Well, first of all, because he said he would. But even that doesn't fully answer it. Because certainly a Being so great could change his mind.

So why did God come to be with us?

The answer is so simple and yet is beyond my understanding. Because the answer to this question truly is the answer to all of our questions. And if we would first live this answer before and above everything else, then our lives would be radically different. This answer is the very reason God came to be with us. And it's something we once knew but we forgot about along the way. And this Emmanuel God tried to remind us throughout the years. He sent folks all over the place to remind us. And often, we'd remember for a while. But then our power of choice and the influence of the Enemy would distract us...and we'd forget. Emmanuel God came to be with us for one reason. What is it? It's so simple...will you believe me when I tell you? Okay, here goes...

Love.

God could not sit idly by watching us hate each other. God could not sit idly by watching us destroy or worse yet, ignore each other. Because truly, the opposite of Love is not hate...it's indifference. And God is not indifferent. God is the very answer he sent...Love.

Emmanuel. God with us.

Love. Love with us.

Mary didn't really understand how with us God would be. Do we?

My friends, Emmanuel is here. God is with us. God is with you at this very moment, wherever you are. God is with you whether or not you even want him to be. God is with you as you walk the malls, searching for that something to fill your Loved one's void. God is with you as you look for things that you think will fill your own void. God is with you at work. God is with you when your work is fulfilling...and when it's not. God is with you when you sin. God is with you even when you turn your back on him. God is with you. *Love* is with you.

Christmas is a reminder to us not of a fairy-tale-esque story of Wise Men, Shepherds and Angels...although the story we read each year at this time does recount the blessing of Emmanuel...and there is great value in reading the Truth, God's Word. No, Christmas is ultimately a reminder that God is with us...that Love is with us.

That is the miracle of Emmanuel. That is the real surprise we receive each Christmas. The real surprise is not a box with ribbons and bows...but is the fact that the Infinite Almighty Creator would choose to enter in not in a blazing chariot of fire, vanquishing our foes, but as a baby, basking in our Love...blessing us with his.

He didn't have to do it, you know. He didn't have to be Emmanuel...God with us. But he did. And each Christmas, we are given the choice of whether or not to receive this gift of Love. Christmas is a bold reminder that Love awaits us in every moment whether we want it or not. That is the miracle...the gift...the great surprise of Emmanuel...God is with us. Love is with us.

Christmas is about what God gave. Not what we give. Will you receive his gift? Will you receive the great gift of Emmanuel this Christmas? Will you open your arms and receive the great gift of God's Love?

He didn't have to do it, you know. But he did.

Will you?

And God Winked

Luke 2: 8-12

There's a light breeze, blowing the tall grass, making whisper noises that foreshadow the song that will be sung later this very same night. The crickets are chirping, adding their harmony to the whisper-song of the grass.

There is a group of shepherds there, reclining in the grass, keepin' an eye on their flock of sheep. Some of them slept, getting some sleep before it came their turn to take shift on the night watch. They probably had a few small campfires going to further scare away predators and to warm up some food. As they camped there, some of them probably wondered about the bright star in the sky. I'll bet some of them even gossiped about it, coming up with possibilities for its purpose. This is a scene, just itchin' to be painted. It's a Kodak moment.

The world in solemn stillness lay. It is a silent night. The midnight is clear. Bethlehem is lying still. All is calm.

For the moment, that is. Little do those poor shepherds know what's coming next.

Sheepherders are prepared for predators. They know that at some point in their illustrious careers tending flocks of sheep, they will have to do hand-to-paw combat with some nasty fang-bearing critter that would enjoy a midnight snack, munching a sheep or two. Sheepherders are prepared for bad weather. They know they'll have to find shelter for themselves and quite possibly weather some bad storms. They're prepared for long times away from family and friends. They're prepared for travel. They're prepared to search for a lost sheep.

But the shepherds we read about in this story were nowhere near prepared for what would break the silent reverie of their midnight clear.

Half-dozing sheepherders, leaning upon their staffs, as the wind whispers through the tall grass are shocked from their peace by an angel that just appears out of nowhere.

I imagine some of them going into attack mode, thinking of protecting their sheep, almost attacking God's messenger. I imagine that some of them were too bewildered to do much of anything, standing there with mouths agape. And I imagine that some of them were so startled that they soiled themselves from the sudden shock of the angel's appearance.

Can you blame them? They didn't have much experience with angels. When they were going to shepherd school, there was no elective course in Angel Appearances and What To Do About Them. The story tells us that they were terrified. I imagine that when the shepherds who went into attack mode or were bewildered truly realized who had just appeared...an angel of the Lord!...that they all became terrified.

I imagine this rough, gnarled group of guys huddling together in fear, knees trembling, some of them begging for mercy, others crying. Have you ever been afraid like this? Have you ever truly been terrified? Because these men were. They were truly terrified. Fear was reducing them to a group of knee-knocking, simpering, whimpering children.

The first words out of the angel's mouth? "Don't be afraid."

Some of them probably thought, "Uh huh. Yeah, right! Don't be afraid? Easy for you to say Mr. Bright-and-shiny-Angel-of-the-Lord-guy. You just pop in out of nowhere and we're supposed to 'not be afraid.' Excuse me while I go clean out my shorts."

But others of them, I'm sure, were able to hear the tone of the angel's voice. They were able to hear the peace there. They were able to hear the words of God through the chaos of this event. These shepherds breathed a sigh of relief. And as their brains began to give way to peace instead of fear, a new thought dawned upon them: "Why on God's green earth are you coming to *us*? We're just a bunch of stinky ol' shepherds out watching our flocks by night. How come you're not visiting that ol' King Herod? Why aren't you going to the priests in the temples? What do you want from us?"

The angel chuckles lightly, adding a note of joy to this chaotic moment. "What do I want from you? I don't want anything from you. That's not why I came. I want something *for* you. I want to tell you some news."

"News? God sends an angel to us to share some news? We don't get it." responds one of the more experienced shepherds.

"It's precisely because you are who you are that God has sent me to you. God's kinda gettin' tired of being so predictable. So, this time around, he's going to mess with things a bit. Instead of sending angels to the people you'd expect, he's sent me to a young virgin and her fiancée, a group of foreign scholars, and you guys! The kings and priests of your world need some shakin' up. So, here I am, talkin' to you...shakin' things up."

The shepherds could appreciate that. They understood the joke. And they suddenly had a whole new appreciation for God. A new joy filled them...although it could also be called humor. And with smiles beginning to appear on their faces as each one of them in turn began to realize how God was upending their social order, one of them asked, "So, what news do you have for us?"

"Are you ready for this?" asked the angel, "You've known for a long time that God was going to send a Messiah, right?"

"Yup." responded the shepherds.

"Well, get this...God's sent the Messiah, all right, but..." the angel had to stop to laugh. He finally got control of himself, took a deep breath, and said, "but the Messiah is a baby!" with that, the angel burst into tears, he began to laugh so hard.

The shepherds didn't quite get it at first. And so one of them asked, "Well, he's like some sort of a king or something, right?"

"Well, yeah. Technically he's a King. But this King has just been born in some motel-stable down there in Bethlehem. And his throne is a smelly old feeding box used for the stable animals. You see, guys, God's not interested in all of the religious trappings. He's tired of all the pomp and circumstance you've added to worshiping him. That's why he sent me to regular folks...unexpected folks. That's why God sent the Messiah as a helpless baby who will grow up with common people. God wants to be known by the least, the last, and the lost, because the most, the first, and the found already know God and have missed the point."

"What's the point?" asked a shepherd.

"The point is this: Love God...Love each other. But you know what...I shouldn't say anymore. I'll let your new Messiah tell you...when he learns how to talk!"

The shepherds all laughed at that.

"Now, just one more thing," said the angel.

"Sure, what's that?" asked the sheepherders.

"God would like you guys to head down to Bethlehem and go see him. He'll be in that stable I was telling you about."

"You got it. We'll go and see him. Anything we need to bring?" they asked.

"Nope...well, nothing material anyway...just bring your sense of humor...and bring your hearts." said the angel.

And so the unlikely heralds of the Messiah went to see him. They laughed and talked along the way. They wondered about the future. They wondered how things would change. They wondered how this Messiah would save them. And they laughed some more at the thought of the Lord of the Universe having such a great sense of humor.

And when they got there, joy exploded from them as they saw the Messiah lying there in that feeding box. The poor virgin and her husband looked tired, but a great sense of peace filled them.

And here is how I imagine the scene to have happened...that as the smelly sheepherders approached, the Baby Messiah King looked at them...God looked at them... and *winked*.

And the sheepherders smiled. And then they knelt to worship him.

The Log Drawer

Luke 2:8-11

It was the Christmas of 1996. And the plan was to visit my mom a couple of days after Christmas at her apartment to celebrate with her. I spoke with her on Christmas Day and she was so excited for us to come over, eat dinner, open gifts, and share the joy of Christmas together. And that year, my sister Kammi was going to be able to be with us as well. We were going to all be together for the first time in several years. Our excitement was tangible.

As we got to that Sunday, I remember the anticipation we all felt as we drove to Anoka, Minnesota, to visit my mom at her apartment. And I remember the look on her face as we all showed up. I remember the tears that welled up in her eyes as we all walked through her door. I remember the smile of purest joy on her face...and the enduring, unyielding hug with which she enveloped me. She didn't want to let go.

She finally loosened her arms, stepped back, wiped the tears from her eyes, and invited me in. She was proud to have us all together in her home. And we were all blessed to be there. After coming in, she offered us something to drink, and she had some Christmas cookies out for us. As I bit into the first one, childhood memories flooded back of sitting at the table with bowls of homemade different colored butter frosting...containers of green and red sugar crystals, red-hots, sprinkles, and those little silver balls to use as stars for the tops of Christmas tree cookies. You know, the ones on which you almost chipped your teeth as a kid. Awesome memories helping to create a beautiful day.

After eating some of mom's home-cooked food, and sharing time together, she was too excited to wait any longer and ushered us into the living room where we gathered around the Christmas tree. Now, this Christmas, I was just glad to get together with her. Financially, she had not been doing that well and so I honestly didn't expect extravagant gifts. But she was quick to prove me wrong. It turns out she had been saving up so she could lavish her children and grandchildren with gifts to show her Love. Cool toys for the children, jewelry, perfume, and clothes for my sister and my wife, and all the while, I sat there in awe of this grand event my mother had created for us, her family.

As I sat there on her floor admiring the extravagance with which my mother was blessing her family, I began to get excited about the gift I saw under the tree for me. I began to speculate about nice cologne, or new clothes, or...

Nothing could prepare me for what was to come next. My mom—the woman who carried me for nine months in her womb—the woman who raised me and knew me better than probably anyone—this woman handed me my gift as the grand finale to her gift-giving extravaganza. And I was excited, because the gift she passed me seemed to have some serious weight to it.

I shredded the paper and what to my wondering eyes should appear?

With bewilderment, I said as I pulled the item from its wrapping: "Oh...it's a log."

But then I turned it around and noticed something more. "Oh...and it has a drawer in it."

My adoring mother had gotten me a log drawer.

And she looked at me with deep meaning in her eyes and said, "When I saw it, I thought of you."

And I couldn't help but almost wonder aloud, "And what, exactly, was it you thought of me?"

A log drawer.

I thanked my mother profusely for this enigmatic gift. And we concluded our holiday festivities together.

The log drawer became a sort of white elephant gift between our friends and us. When friends would come and stay, we would sneak the log drawer into their luggage before they left. And upon arriving home, we would receive a phone call asking, "Why do we have a log drawer?" And so it would go, the log drawer passing back and forth.

Years later, the log drawer disappeared from my possession. I'm not exactly certain of its ultimate destination. Maybe it's still in someone's old suitcase in the back of a closet somewhere. But I know that I don't have the log drawer any longer.

After mom passed away right before Christmas in 2001, I would remember the log drawer each Christmas. And in fact, when I think of the many gifts I'd like to receive, there is no other gift I'd rather have than that puzzling piece of timber with the drawer carved into it.

The log drawer. I never understood it, or the reason my mom got it for me. But I can't help but think that in some way, I need it.

Sometimes, the gifts we understand the least, are the ones we need the most.

And so it is, the extravagant gift of Love comes to us, not in ways we could expect...nor in ways we can understand...but in a smelly sheep cave.

A smelly sheep cave. The birthplace of Grace.

When I think of the log drawer and of my mother, I know I have no understanding of the gift—but I know the giver. And I know how much she Loved me.

And so it is when I allow myself each Christmas to go to the manger scene...the smelly sheep cave...I can't help but wonder what the Almighty was thinking when he chose not to ride in with a flaming chariot to save us all, but rather, chose to be born as a diaper-wearing infant in a smelly sheep cave.

Sometimes, the gifts we understand the least, are the ones we need the most.

I can't understand the gift of Grace itself...let alone the way in which it came to us. But I know I need it.

I know that on a daily basis, I fall short. I fall short of my expectations for myself. I fall short of my family's expectations for me. I fall short at work, and at home, and with my friends. I miss the mark all the time. And yet, God shows up in the smelliness of my life, and Loves on me extravagantly, justifying me with his Grace...clothing me in his righteousness.

I don't understand it. But I know I need it.

As you gather with friends or family this Christmas, and as you tear into the wrapping paper, I'm sure you will find at least one present under the tree that you don't fully understand.

But remember this: you know the giver. You know their Love for you.

And so while you may not understand the gift...you know the heart of the giver.

And so it is with grace...with Jesus. We can't possibly fully understand the gift...but we know the heart of the Giver.

Sometimes, dear friend, the gifts we understand the least, are the ones we need the most.

By the way, if you happen to find the log drawer, would you mind returning it? I promise it won't end up in your luggage ever again. It will be put in a place where I can see it everyday and be reminded of the heart of the one who gave it to me...and through hers, the Father's as well.

Merry Christmas to you, dear friend.

EPILOGUE:
UNCONTAINABLE SERENADE

The attractive young sprite of a brunette with a rich voice like caramel is being serenaded by a special-needs gentleman in his late fifties in the coffee shop. Jazz music plays in the background, reverberating off the original tin ceiling, the serenade a juxtaposition of harmonic dissonance. His vocal abilities are questionable and atonal at best. And yet his Love adds harmony and depth to my morning.

He is ass-over-teakettle in Love with her. He's even purchased flowers for the lass. He is likely old enough to be her grandfather. His song is interrupted by a customer asking for his spiced Chai tea latte to be reheated.

"I should stop. I'm causing a ruckus," he says.

The sprite allows the man his dignity. She chokes back laughter, allowing only a smile that could be interpreted either as mockery, or appreciation. Thankfully, the gentleman sees only appreciation.

He returns to his seat, his serenade still in mid-composition. He is sporting a Discman. I've not seen its like in years. And with coffee being slung, customers streaming in from the snow, said jazz continuing to play, I sit in the next booth behind the balladeer, listening to him compose new lines to his expressions of affection.

It is a beautiful moment in the chaos of life.

For isn't this all about Love?

Life is about Love. And this man is feelin' it. It is a burning fire within him, uncontainable, like re-packing springy snakes from a false can of peanuts, his Love will not go back in. It's out there. Bursting forth for all to witness.

Life can be like that, I think—Love bursting forth for all to witness.

Someone's windshield being cleared of ice and snow as a surprise, another's coffee tab being paid secretly, a family in need being blessed by a group of friends, pooling their resources to purchase coats for cold little girls, and socks for their older brother, a God who would choose to enter into the fray as a helpless child.

Untamed, uncontainable Love bursting forth.

May it be so for you, friend. I hope that through these pages, Love has burst forth for you in some way.

May Love burst forth in your life. And may you be Love bursting forth in someone else's.

For we need more of that. Don't ya think?

Untamed,
Shane Allen Burton

ABOUT THE AUTHOR

*S*hane has been a pastor in both established churches and church plants throughout his 21 years of ministry. For much of that time, he was a pastor in the United Methodist Church, including one church plant, but also led a Baptist congregation, a non-denominational church plant, and has been a worship leader at Hastings United Methodist Church, Fridley Covenant Church, and New Day United Methodist Church.

He has worked as a pastor, insurance agent, pawn broker, mortgage broker, executive director of a publishing company, supervisor in an oil refinery, editor, and most recently as a Family Services Counselor for several cemeteries. He currently resides in Andover, Minnesota and has four children: Patrick 20, Tucker 17, Darby 15, and Zander 11.

Shane loves good coffee, fine chocolate (*any* chocolate, for that matter), reading books, Grand Adventures, writing, editing, musical performance (drums, guitar, vocals), and composition. His child-like, untamed faith is contagious and you will notice in church his complete inability to be still!

CPSIA information can be obtained
at www.ICGtesting.com
Printed in the USA
BVHW070855211120
593810BV00010B/505